## The First Bridge Book

Jeremy Flint was World Master of the World Bridge Federation, Grand Master of the English Bridge Union and Life Master of the American Contract Bridge League. He had competed in numerous international bridge tournaments and wrote, or co-authored, ten other bridge books. He was bridge correspondent to *The Times* for over ten years and appeared, both as player and as commentator, in the television series *Grand Slam* and *Bridge Club*, a series for beginners.

John Gullick taught bridge to many thousands of beginners and founded the Wimbledon Bridge Club.

JEREMY FLINT and JOHN GULLICK

# The First Bridge Book

ROBERT HALE • LONDON

© Jeremy Flint and John Gullick 1984
First published in Great Britain 1984
Reprinted 1986, 1987, 1989, 1991 and 1994
Reprinted with corrections 1997

ISBN 0 7090 5457 2

Robert Hale Limited
Clerkenwell House
Clerkenwell Green
London EC1R OHT

10 9 8 7 6 5 4 3

Printed by Gutenberg Press Limited, Malta

# Contents

# Preface

by JEREMY FLINT and JOHN GULLICK

Victorian parents taught their children to wash their hands before meals, clean their teeth twice a day, speak only when spoken to, and – above all – not to frighten the horses. As the children grew up they retained some of these pieces of advice, discarded others as no longer appropriate, and deliberately flouted the rest because they curtailed their enjoyment of life.

This is our approach to beginning bridge. In Part 1 we offer positive directions, most of which you will need to retain for as long as you play. In Part 2, as you grow into bridge, we begin to discard and amend some of our advice, and even hint at how it can sometimes be flouted.

This allows us to present a guide with a minimum of asterisks, footnotes and other irritating interruptions, in a framework that does not require you to undertake a mass of learning before you can handle the cards.

It is directed at beginners but goes much further than most books for beginners, so will also be of value to the thousands who enjoy their bridge but have a feeling that they really ought not to be making so many mistakes! They will need to skip only the introduction.

To them we would say that we are following the Acol system of bidding, but in fact Acol is not, and never was, a system. It originated in Britain as a revolt against the extreme doctrinaire approach of the Americans, and proclaimed the benefits of natural bidding. It was an ideology rather than a system.

However, it soon became so undoctrinaire as to verge on anarchy, so that rules had to be added. Over the years it was mulled over by experts, finely honed and frequently amended so that the Acol of today bears no more resemblance to the original than the golfer's old gutty ball does to the whizzing projectile of modern times.

What we teach in this book is the refined product, a natural method of bidding, inside tight guidelines but at the same time allowing for extreme flexibility.

A glossary of bridge terminology will be found at the end of this book.

# Preface

by JOHN GULLICK

Bridge is fun, which is why so many people play it. Learning should be fun too, and this, I hope, is reflected in the way *The First Bridge Book* is written.

Beginners are often put off by the mass of material they are asked to assimilate before they can get down to the game. Our book is so designed that you can join in the action as early as the end of Chapter 1.

Of course, beginners vary in the ease with which they pick up the game. You may find it easy, or not so easy. It doesn't seem to depend on IQ, profession (or lack of profession), or sex. It is unimportant anyway. I know from experience that all beginners are going to hesitate in the same places and find certain advice difficult to remember. Because of this, Jeremy Flint and I have adopted a system unique to this book. Passages marked with daggers are those likely to be the stumbling blocks on your journey to proficiency. At three daggers you are looking at points which nearly all beginners have a struggle to remember. You have been warned!

I want to mention one other matter here. One or two of our bids vary from conventional teaching. This is not an attempt to be 'modern'. For a long time good players have bid one way and beginners have been taught another. We see no reason for continuing the paradox.

But do not be alarmed that we are sending you out into the world with a system at odds with everyone else's, so that you become a bridge-playing pariah. It won't matter in the least if you bid our way and your partner another. The differences are slight, but significant, and will make the game easier for you and more rewarding.

# Preface

by JEREMY FLINT

The reader is always entitled to question the justification for joint authorship. Is the product the result of two writers' harmonious collaboration? Or is one of the names there only to invest the book with an air of extra authority?

Although I have done many things in the bridge world, my experience of teaching beginners is limited to one occasion many years ago. A beguiling girl asked if I would give her some bridge lessons. The tuition did not run its appointed course. It was terminated, as the popular newspapers would put it, 'on the most amicable terms'.

John Gullick, on the other hand, has taught countless beginners. He has learned from experience how to lighten the blind spots and to explain simple things so that they appear simple.

My contribution is this. Bridge theory has changed considerably in the last thirty years, and this change has not generally been reflected in books for beginners. Some of those written by accepted authorites are old and insufficiently revised. Others recite the old doctrines – fallacies and all.

On any theme there may sometimes be a case for proffering the opinion of two plausible schools of thought; equally there are times when a previously accepted notion is demonstrably wrong. In bridge: 'bid the higher of two touching four-card suits'. Wrong! 'With a 4-4-4-1 fit, bid the suit below the singleton.' Rubbish! 'Double a weak no trump on 14pts.' Suicide!

Although the *First Bridge Book* is an elementary book, you may rest assured that the basic principles we track are those practised by the leading players in the land.

John Gullick will teach you how to stand and how to grip the club. I will try to ensure that you use the best clubs on the market.

# Introduction: beginning bridge

Bridge is the most fascinating of card games. It is played by millions around the world, from top internationals to families and friends in their own homes. It is a social asset and a route to new friendships. It is immensely varied; the cards you pick up after each deal will never be the same, so many are the possible combinations.

Above all, bridge is fun.

The late Iain Macleod wrote a book entitled *Bridge is an Easy Game*. He was right, though you may doubt it in the early stages. There appears to be a bewildering amount of information to assimilate, but don't worry. Take it stage by stage and let the picture form gradually.

As in any field of activity the basic principles are all-important. The most brilliant mathematician had to start by being taught that 2 and 2 make 4; a concert pianist has first to learn the scales, a golfer how to grip a golf club.

It is true that bridge can be enjoyed at any level. However, the better you become, the more enjoyable it is – and that means a sure foundation.

If you can take a grasp on the early lessons, with some practice you will probably become as good a player as most of your friends – quite possibly better.

Bridge really is an easy game – if you put some effort into learning the fundamentals of bidding and play.

A pack of cards contains thirteen of each of four suits: spades, hearts, diamonds and clubs. The highest card in a suit is the ace, followed by the king, queen, jack, 10 (these five are called the honours) down to the 2.

Bridge is a game for four players, who form two partnerships (the mechanics of beginning a game are described at the end of this preamble). Your partner is your ally in a contest against the other two players.

One of the four deals the cards clockwise, face down, one at a time, so that each player ends with thirteen cards. You arrange these in suits in your hand.

Now bridge can be divided into two distinct parts. Firstly, the *bidding* (or calling). Secondly, the *play* in which both sides try to make as many tricks as possible.

We will concentrate first on *tricks*.

## Tricks

In the play which follows the bidding, one player *leads* a card, and the other three *play* a card, following suit. The four cards constitute a trick, and there will ultimately be thirteen on the table. The highest card wins a trick, but a player unable to follow suit may throw away a card in another suit – or play a trump, which beats everything else (except a higher trump).

As an example, suppose one suit is divided in the four hands like this:

$$\begin{array}{ccc} & J75 & \\ AKQ2 & \boxed{\phantom{XX}} & 863 \\ & 1094 & \end{array}$$

The East–West partnership is going to take four tricks (assuming no trumps are around). The ace, then the king, then the queen are led out, and the other three players follow three times. That will be twelve cards played, so the remaining little 2 in West's hand becomes a fourth trick.

And, because bridge is a partnership game, the result will be exactly the same if the cards are divided like this:

$$\begin{array}{ccc} & J75 & \\ AQ62 & \boxed{\phantom{XX}} & K83 \\ & 1094 & \end{array}$$

Now East and West both contribute to the taking of four tricks.

But if we put one more card in the West hand, and one fewer in East's:

$$\begin{array}{ccc} & J75 & \\ AQ862 & \boxed{\phantom{XX}} & K3 \\ & 1094 & \end{array}$$

East and West together are going to take five tricks, because there is a five-card suit in one hand. From this you can see that taking tricks depends on a combination of high cards and length of suit.

At the beginning you will find it helpful to put down four hands face upwards and play from each one in turn. It is crucial to understand how the cards fall, and how many tricks are to be won or lost.

**The bidding**

The dealer has the right to make the first bid, followed by the player on dealer's left and so on, clockwise round the table.

With a poor hand you do not bid. You say, 'No bid'. With a reasonable hand (what constitutes this is explained later) you open the bidding, naming your best suit as trumps. As a trump beats any other card, the more you have the better. Your opponents may compete in their suit, and so it continues until one partnership drops out.

Your objective is to bid up to the number of tricks which you can make in the play which follows.

Most bidding opens with one of a suit. If you open, for example, one spade, you are saying:

● that, for the moment at least, you want spades to be trumps, and
● that you hope to take seven tricks.

*All bids have an unspoken six tricks in the background*: so one spade means one plus six tricks; three spades means three plus six tricks, etc.

Apart from naming a trump suit, the other type of bid you can make is no trumps, which is exactly that – a bid saying you will play the hand without a trump suit.

*All bids must be higher than the one before,* so now you must know their ranking order. With the most senior at the top they are:

| | |
|---|---|
| NTs | no trumps |
| ♠ | spades |
| ♡ | hearts |
| ◇ | diamonds |
| ♣ | clubs |

For instance, after a bid of one heart, the next call can be one spade or 1NT, but a call in diamonds or clubs (lower in the pecking order) has to be two diamonds or two clubs. And so the bidding continues until the final bid is made; that is, the one which is followed by three 'no bids'. The final bid becomes the 'contract'.

**The play**

Let us suppose that the contract is four hearts. Whichever of the two partners first bid hearts – we'll say it was you – now becomes 'declarer' and assumes total command. From now on your partner is a nonentity, known as 'dummy', and takes no further part in the proceedings. You are going to play both hands, yours and dummy's, and try to make ten tricks (four plus six) with hearts as trumps.

The opponent on your left leads the first card – known as the opening lead – and then dummy's hand is spread face upwards on the table with trumps on the right.

You follow suit from dummy to the card led, then your right-hand opponent plays, and finally you (again everything goes clockwise). Whoever wins the trick, either with the highest card in the suit or with a trump, gathers it together and begins a stack for that side. The winner of the trick then leads to trick two, and so on until the hand is over. At the end, you may have made your ten tricks or you may not have done.

If you did, you scored a game. If you failed, you gave away a penalty score to your opponents. There, in a nutshell, is a hand of bridge – the deal, the bidding, the play and the result.

Your first objective is to make a game. Your ultimate aim is to win a rubber, which is the best of three games. How you accomplish this is explained by the scoresheet on page 16. At this stage we are not going to burden you with all the details of scoring, but you need to know some in order to understand what you are trying to do.

| We | They |
| --- | --- |
|  |  |
|  |  |
|  |  |
|  |  |

A game is made by scoring 100 points. A trick in each suit has a value attached to it: clubs and diamonds are worth 20pts each, hearts and spades 30pts each, and no trumps 40pts for the first trick and 30pts for subsequent tricks.

So if you bid and make 1♣ (seven tricks) you enter 30 on the scoresheet. It goes below the line drawn across the middle of the page.

Now do some simple multiplication. You will see that, in order to top the 100 mark and score a game, you need to bid and make:

5 clubs or 5 diamonds (5 × 20)   11 tricks
4 hearts or 4 spades (4 × 30)   10 tricks
3 no trumps (40 + 30 + 30)   9 tricks

You may also acquire your game by degrees. 2♠ bid and made are 60. Only 40 is now needed to complete the 100.

The important feature in a scoresheet is the central line. *Everything you bid and make goes below the line, and this is where the rubber is won and lost.*

| We | They |
|-----|------|
|     |      |
|     |      |
|     |      |
|     |      |
|     |      |
|     |      |
|     |      |
| 120 | 60   |
|     | 60   |
|     | 60   |
|     |      |
|     |      |
|     |      |
|     |      |
|     |      |

On the left a scoresheet gets under way. You enter your own scores under 'We' and your opponents' under 'They'.

In the first deal your opponents bid 2♡ and made the required eight tricks. That is 60pts (2 × 30) below the line to 'They'.

Next time you and your partner picked up good hands with plenty of spades. Between you you bid to 4♠ and made your ten tricks. That is 120 (4 × 30) to you and your partner, 'We', below the line. A line is drawn under it to show that a game has been won and that your opponents' part score of 60 no longer counts towards game.

Your opponents won the third hand with 3◇, 60pts (3 × 20), and the next with 2♡, 60pts (2 × 30). The two scores added together gave them the second game.

And so on, until one side wins the deciding game and the rubber.

Those are the only scores which go below the line; what you bid and make. Everything else goes above.

Above-the-line scores have no bearing on who wins the rubber. They are for penalties, overtricks and honours – which you will learn about later – and are totted up after the rubber is over; then one column is deducted from the other and a final outcome reached.

Your objective in bridge is to bid accurately up to the number of tricks you can make, because:

- if you bid too little (underbid) you do not reap the reward. 2♠ bid and 4♠ made scores you not a game but only 60pts towards it. The other 60pts for overtricks goes above the line;
- if you bid too high (overbid) you don't score anything at all; on the contrary you give away a penalty to your opponents, scored above the line.

| We | They |
|---|---|
| | |
| | 100[3] |
| 60[6] | |
| 300[5] | 50[1] |
| | |
| | |
| 120[2] | |
| | |
| | 100[4] |
| 60[6] | |
| 40[7] | |
| 500[8] | |
| 1080 | 250 |

Here is a completed scoresheet. You may like to study it, but if you wish you may skip the page and return to it at a later stage.

In this rubber, you first went down by one trick and lost 50pts[1]. In the next hand, you made the first game with 4♡ (120pts)[2]. You draw a line under this to show that a game has been won.

Once a partnership has won a game it becomes what is known as 'vulnerable'. Now the penalties increase sharply; this is why you lost 100pts[3] when you went one down on the next hand.

Your opponents next called and made 3NT (100pts)[4]. Game to them, game all, and both sides vulnerable.

In the next hand, your opponents, bidding much too high, went three down. 300pts to you[5].

After this you bid 2♠ and made ten tricks (two overtricks), 60pts below the line and 60pts above[6], and followed it the hand after with 2◇ (40pts)[7]. Now you have the second game and the rubber.

You score a bonus of 500pts for winning the rubber[8] (700 if in straight games). Now tot up the two columns and subtract one from the other. 1080pts to you, 250 to your opponents. Result: 830pts to you, which to the nearest 100 is 800.

Before the rubber begins you have agreed a stake – perhaps 1p a 100, perhaps £1 a 100. Depending on your stake, you have won 8p or £8.

*Remember:* it is what you bid and make that goes towards the game. If you bid 2♠ and make 4♠, only 60 goes below the line. The other 60 joins the sundries above the line.

The preliminaries end here. What you must memorize so far:

- *The ranking of suits* (from the top): no trumps, spades, hearts, diamonds, clubs; and the fact that each bid must be higher than the one before.
- *The values of the suits*: 20pts for clubs and diamonds; 30pts for hearts and spades; in no trumps, 40 pts for the first trick and 30pts for subsequent tricks.

**The mechanics of beginning a rubber**

A pack is spread face downwards on the table, and the four players each turn over a card. The two with the highest cards play together as partners. (This is 'cutting for partners'.)

If two cards of the same denomination are cut, the ranking of the suits decides. For instance, the ten of spades, the six of hearts, the six of clubs and the three of clubs; hearts are higher than clubs, so the six of hearts and the ten of spades are partners.

The player cutting the highest card has the choice of seats and packs (usually red or blue). The choice is irrelevant, but many people have a superstitious bias towards a particular seat or colour.

The player cutting the highest card also becomes the dealer of the first hand. The pack is shuffled by the player on dealer's left and passed to the dealer (who may, but does not often, shuffle again) and then to the player on dealer's right, who cuts the cards. Dealer completes the cut and deals.

All this rigmarole, of the cards passing through three sets of hands, is to foil the villainous card sharp who, left to himself, knows how to shuffle all the aces into his hand. Although you are not likely to encounter him, it has all become standard procedure.

And while this is going on, dealer's partner shuffles the other pack and puts it on the right, ready for the next deal.

If at any stage of reading this book you wish to refresh your memory on bridge terminology, please refer to the glossary at the end.

# Part 1
# Making a start

# 1  Simple bidding

The deal is made. You sort your cards into suits. Now comes the decision whether or not to open the bidding. It is an easy one.

---

*How to value your hand*

A system of points is used.

An ace is allotted 4pts, a king 3pts, a queen 2pts and a jack 1pt.
†You open the bidding with 13pts or more.

If the points are equally divided and no player has an opening bid, the cards are thrown in and the next in order deals.

---

If you have 13pts or more, you bid your best suit by saying 1♠, 1♡, 1◇, or 1♣.

Now, this is not just an idle announcement of the points in your hand. It is a message to your partner, 'I have at least 13pts and I suggest spades (or whatever) as trumps. What about it?'

In return your partner sends a message back to you. It may be a depressing one, a no bid, signifying a miserable hopeless hand; it may be one agreeing with you that spades should be trumps; even an alternative proposal of another suit; or yet another that the hand should be played without a trump suit – in no trumps.

What you are doing is transmitting and receiving information, so that each partner can build up a picture of the other's hand.

The messages are very short, like this:

1 spade – 1 no trump

That is all you are allowed, two or three words at the most, more like a staccato telegram than a letter.

But you can communicate an awful lot in three words – 'I love you' says it all; 'Go to blazes' is a complete message; 'Arriving home tomorrow'; 'Your terms agreed', and so on.

Actually, while bidding at bridge you would really like to send a much longer message, describing your hand in full. However, you cannot; so in the space allowed you need to be as helpful and illuminating to your partner as you can. What you are trying to do between you is to find out:

● which suit should be trumps, or whether to play in no trumps;
● how high to go – whether to bid to game or to stop short.

Here is a guide:

---

You need about 25/26pts in total in your hand and your partner's to play in 3NT
You need about 26pts in total in your hand and your partner's to play 4♡ or 4♠
You need about 28/29pts in total in your hand and your partner's to play 5♣ or 5◇

These are the game bids; with fewer points you should stop short.

---

Playing in a suit you should have eight trumps at least between the two hands.

---

Throughout the following pages the suits are shown in their order of seniority:

♠ spades
♡ hearts
◇ diamonds
♣ clubs

An x denotes a small card number under 10

This is standard, but we are going to add some symbols of our own. From experience we know the bids and cardplays which beginners find most difficult to remember. These will be marked with daggers, (†††) one, two or three, according to the likelihood of your having a mental stumble.

Take special note of the dagger passages, and be pleased each time you have assimilated one of them. You will be on your way.

*Opener*

With 13pts or more, open one of a suit. Count extra points for length of suits, 1pt for every card over four cards in a suit, i.e.:

♠AQx    6pts
♡xx      −
◇KJ      4
♣Axxxxx  4 plus 2: total 16pts. Open 1♣

Now here are the opening bids to make on the      †
various combinations of cards you may pick up. The first is easy: *Always* open your longest suit:

♠xxxxx   1pt (for length)
♡AKQx    9
◇KJx     4
♣x       −    total 14pts. Open 1♠.

Don't worry about the lack of honours in spades; if the suit becomes trumps, its length is more important than how pretty the cards in it are.

Whenever your hand contains suits of equal length:

1  with two four-card suits, open the lower:

♠Ax
♡KJxx
◇Qxx
♣AJxx            open 1♣

**2** with two five-card or two six-card suits, open the higher, *except* when holding clubs and spades; then open 1♣:

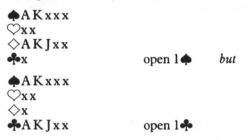

♠AKxxx
♡xx
◇AKJxx
♣x                    open 1♠        *but*

♠AKxxx
♡xx
◇x
♣AKJxx               open 1♣

**3** with three four-card suits open 1♣, *but* when your three suits are touching, open the middle one. Suits touch in order of their hierarchy, i.e. spades touch hearts, hearts touch diamonds, diamonds touch clubs.

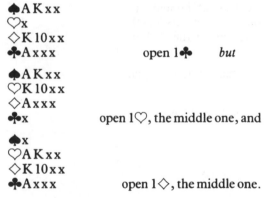

♠AKxx
♡x
◇K10xx
♣Axxx                open 1♣        *but*

♠AKxx
♡K10xx
◇Axxx
♣x                   open 1♡, the middle one, and

♠x
♡AKxx
◇K10xx
♣Axxx                open 1◇, the middle one.

These few lines contain all the possible combinations of cards which can be dealt to you: one suit longer than the others, two suits of equal length; three four-card suits. But just two further notes:

- Still to come is an opening bid of 1NT, on hands containing exactly 12–14pts and no 5-card suit or singleton. Ignore such hands until you reach Chapter 6.

● Do you ask *why* you open the bidding differently on four- and five-card suits? The answer is that your opening bid carries a promise to bid again if required (from Chapter 3 onwards). Your first bid, therefore, is tailored to make your second bid as easy as possible.

● Many opening bids are made on less than 13pts. See various references later.

### Responder

Now make a mental switch. You have become the partner of the opening bidder, known in bridge parlance as the 'responder'. An ugly word, but there it is; everyone uses it.

As responder you reply to your partner's opening bid with a bid of your own if you have 6pts or more. With fewer, pass with a no bid. This is *not* optional: with 6pts plus, bid!          †

As responder you *can only* make one of three bids, other than a no bid:

1 support your partner's suit;
2 bid NTs; (these are the *limit bids*)
3 bid another suit (to come in Chapter 3).

The *limit bids* are just what they sound like. You bid the limit of your hand in one go. So, divide your hand into three categories:

6–10pts – minimum
10–12pts – intermediate
13–15pts – strong
(For very strong hands of 16pts plus, see Chapter 7.)

Then

1 support your partner's suit directly (i.e. opening 1♠ – response 2♠) when you have four or more cards in it. (Remember opener can bid a four-card suit; your four will guarantee the necessary eight trumps.) And count extra points for shortages in your hand:

3pts for a void (none of a suit)
2pts for a singleton (one of a suit)
1pt for a doubleton (two of a suit)

(Opening 1♠): with four or more spades and
                      6–10pts bid 2♠;
                   with four or more spades and
                      11–12pts bid 3♠;
                   with four or more spades and
                      13–15pts bid 4♠.

*Example:* ♠Qxxx    2pts
           ♡xx      1pt (for doubleton)
           ◇AKx     7pts
           ♣Jxxx    1pt
           _____
           11pts    bid 3♠

2 Not having four cards in your partner's suit, reply in no trumps. Do not count extra for shortages.

with 6–10pts bid 1 NT;
with 11–12pts bid 2NT;
with 13–15pts bid 3NT.

*Example:* ♠Qxx     2pts
           ♡xxx     –
           ◇AKx     7pts
           ♣Qxxx    2pts
           _____
           11pts    bid 2NT

If this seems like a surfeit of figures, let's put it another way. You are dealing in limits, as you do in everyday life. If you exceed the speed limit (and are apprehended) you will suffer a fine. If you exceed your points limit at bridge, the chances are that you will suffer a penalty.

The parallel is not a true one, for nothing happens to a motorist who goes too slowly (although we often think it should). In bridge this is not so; you suffer if you underbid your points, so you need to be exact. It isn't difficult. Broadly speaking, the better you are, the higher you bid. Precisely how high is determined by the figures above.

*Opener*
It is your turn now. You do not *have* to reply to a limit bid; your options are to pass or bid higher.

You are now involved in simple arithmetic. You have *heard* how many points your partner has, and you can *see* your own. If together they amount to the 26pts needed for game, bid it; if they are some way towards it, make another bid; if they don't add up to much, say no bid.

Specifically, your second bid (your rebid) can be summarized like this:

Responder has made a single raise, 1♠–2♠ or 1♠–1NT

With 13–16pts you have a weak opening: say no bid (but see Chapters 3 and 14).
With 17–18pts you are better: bid again*.
With 19–20pts you are strong: bid game*.

Responder makes a double raise, 1♠–3♠ or 1♠–2NT

With 13–14pts you are still weak: say no bid.
With 15pts plus you can add up to 26: bid game*.

*For the time being your rebids will only be in:
1  your own suit, if partner has raised it, or
2  no trumps.

These opening bids and responses can be expressed in a table:

---

*Opener*
With 13–20pts, bid 1 of a suit, choosing

1 the longest suit, or
2 if suits are of equal length:
  • the lower of two four-card suits;
  • the higher of two five- or six-card suits but 1♣
    if they are clubs and spades;
  • with three four-card suits, the middle one if
    they touch, otherwise 1♣.

> *Responder*
> (After an opening bid from partner: suppose it to be
> 1♡):
>
> with less than 6pts: no bid;
> with 6–10pts bid 2♡ (with four or more hearts) or
> 1NT (without);
> with 11–12pts bid 3♡ (with four or more hearts) or
> 2NT (without);
> with 13–15pts bid 4♡ (with four or more hearts) or
> 3NT (without).

*Opener's rebid*
To a *single* raise, pass on 13–16pts (but see Chapter 3);
                     bid again on 17–18pts;
                     bid game on 19–20pts.

To a *double* raise, pass on 13–14pts;
                     bid game on 15pts plus.

> *Responder's rebid*
> No bid (but see Chapter 3).
> Your first response was a limit bid. Unless you have
> discovered an extra ace on the floor you have already
> reached your limit.

---

In the early stages, keep this table in front of you; with its help you will bid accurately to the correct level. But memorize it as quickly as you can. The categories of points for opener and responder will guide you for the whole of your bridge-playing life.

We are dealing in simple arithmetic. You don't need an abacus to count up to 26.

- Opener bids one of a suit with 13pts and now, if responder also has 13pts – bingo, that is 26pts in the two hands – responder bids the game.
- Opener bids one of a suit with 16pts, and responder bids 2NT with 11pts. Bingo again, opener can add 16 to 11 and come to a game bid.

You deduce from this that Acol limit bids are very precise, and you are right:

| | |
|---|---|
| 1♠ (13 or more pts) | 3♠ (11–12pts and four spades at |
| No bid (13–14pts only) | least) |
| *or* | |
| 1♠ | 2NT (11–12pts, not four spades) |
| 3NT (15pts) | |
| *or* | |
| 1♠ | 2♠ (6–10pts, and four spades at |
| 4♠ (19–20pts) | least) |

But be clear from the start that bidding is not just a parrot-like recital †††
of figures. It is an exchange of information. When your partner bids,
you listen to the message, fit it into your hand and take action
accordingly. When, later on, factors other than points will have to be
considered, it becomes even more crucial for you to realize that you
are only half a partnership. Record that fact now, and remember it for
as long as you play.

### Vital information

When you bid a suit you are initially proposing it as trumps. It follows
that you must have at least reasonable cards in it. As an extreme case,
to suggest as trumps a suit in which you have 5432 would be
ludicrous. So these are the minimum holdings you need to bid a suit,
as opener or responder:

Four-card suits: A x x x, K x x x, Q J x x, Q 10 x x, J 10 x x (but see
p:156); these are biddable, but you may never bid a four-card suit
twice (rebid it) unless your partner has supported it.

Five-card suits: any five-card suit is biddable and rebiddable.

Three-card suits are not biddable at all, either by opener or
responder.

*Reminder no. 1:* Don't forget who you are! If you *began* the bidding
you are the *opener*. If you *replied* to your partner's bid you are the
*responder*.

*Reminder no. 2:* Opener adds extra points for length, responder for shortages.

*Notes:* Chapter 3 will explain why the points ranges 6–10 and 10–12 are duplicated. Chapter 6 deals with opening bids of 1NT.

Perhaps you would find it easier if some everyday product were substituted for points – petrol for instance.

For a journey of 400 miles you know that your (plainly very thirsty) car will swallow 26 gallons. You are going at dead of night through uncharted territory where no filling stations are open.

You have some petrol, of course, but not enough. You call a friend and ask for help. 'By all means,' replies your friend and partner, 'I have 10 or 12 gallons.'

Now count how much *you* have, exactly. Only 13 gallons, and 13 plus 10 or 12 simply will not add up to 26 gallons. That is fact, not surmise. You'll run out of petrol short of your destination. Be safe and bivouac at 300 miles.

Now translate this into

| | |
|---|---|
| 1♠ – 13pts at least | 3♠ – 11–12pts (and four spades) |
| No bid – 13pts only, and 4♠ | |
| is beyond reach | |

(Had your own count been, say, 16pts instead of 13, your final sum would easily have reached 26 and journey's end.)

Or, suppose you are making a plum pie. You need 26 plums to feed four people (the authors are quite uncertain of the culinary quantity, but no matter). The greengrocer is shut, so you call your friend.

'Sorry, I haven't enough. But I've quite a few other fruits, 3 damsons, 3 strawberries – 13 altogether. Why not change your mind and have a mixed fruit pie instead?'

| | |
|---|---|
| 1♠ – 13pts at least | 3NT – 13–15pts |
| | (other goodies but not four spades) |
| | total 26–28pts |
| *or* | |
| | ('Sorry, I'm clean out of every- |
| 1♠ – 13pts at least | thing.') |
| | No bid |

Limits are absolute. They are not subjects for speculation or gambling. As the philosopher (nearly) said: they exist, therefore they are.

Most readers will not thank us if we shovel great chunks of learning down their throats. It is this that daunts many beginners, and sadly puts some of them off bridge for life. We believe that the most interesting way to learn the game is to assimilate some knowledge, and then begin to play. Even at this stage you will find it profitable to handle the cards.

So each chapter will end with a *State of play*.

We suggest that you deal, and then rearrange the cards so that you are not faced with combinations that are ahead of your current state of knowledge. It will not matter at this stage if you see each other's cards.

**State of play**

Deal the cards and rearrange them so that:

- one player has an opening bid with spades as trumps: maximum points 19;
- responder has no five-card suit, and may reply only in spades, in no trumps, or with a no bid: maximum points 15;
- bidding is confined to opener's suit and no trumps;
- no one at the table has a suit with more than six cards in it;
- only one partnership bids; the other, no matter what it holds, stays silent. Now bid and play.
- It will become easier after Chapter 3!

This supposes that four people are learning together. You can manage with three, because during the play the missing fourth can be dummy.

If you are reading this book alone you will find it most helpful to deal the cards, arrange them on the lines above, bid two hands, and then gauge whether or not you were likely to make your contract.

# 2 Play: understanding the cards

The bidding is over; a card has been led; dummy is spread on the table. Now you have to try to make your contract.

Say it is 4♠. You need ten tricks with spades as trumps.

Now pause, and assess your hand with dummy's. 'Marry' them together and see where their joint strengths and weaknesses lie. Look at each suit in turn. Count your winners, the number of immediate winning cards you have: try to count your losers:

♠xxx
♡xxx
♢KQJ
♣Axxx

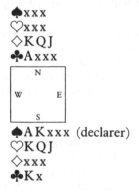

♠AKxxx (declarer)
♡KQJ
♢xxx
♣Kx

†† Many beginners fail to combine the two hands, treating them instead as two separate entities, each with its own existence. If they were, on the hand above you would reckon to lose three small spades in each hand.

But this isn't so, as will be apparent if you remember how the cards fall. Each trick consists of a card from your hand, one from dummy, and one from each of the defenders.

Assuming that the spades are divided in the most likely way, three in one hand and two in the other, thus:

```
     x x x
Q x x  ⬜  J x
     A K x x x
```

the play will go like this:

|  | x |  | x |  | x |
|---|---|---|---|---|---|
| Trick 1 | x⬜x | Trick 2 | x⬜J | Trick 3 | Q⬜– |
|  | A |  | K |  | x |

You have taken two tricks and lost one. Eleven cards have been played, the opponents have none left, and the two small spades left in your hand are two more tricks.

The outcome is that you lose one trick and make four.

Now look again at the two complete hands. After the spades, you need only play the heart king and knock out a defender's ace to take the next two tricks in that suit. The same applies to the diamonds.

In the club suit, you have the king and one little one in your hand and the ace and some others in dummy. The small ones in dummy are not losers because after taking two tricks with the ace and king you have no more left in your hand and can trump any further clubs if necessary.

Your assessment of the two hands, therefore, is: 'I shall lose one spade, the heart ace, the diamond ace and no clubs – three tricks. So I shall take ten tricks, making my contract of 4♠ with four spades, two hearts, two diamonds and two clubs.'

That is the right way, the only way, to approach a hand as declarer. †††
*Count your tricks* before you begin to play.

The exercise of counting winners and losers suit by suit will be slow at first, but it will become quicker. Eventually you will be able to sum up most hands in a few seconds' glance.

You will also very quickly discover that high cards add up to only some of the tricks you need. They are the caviare of your hand; but who can live on caviare alone?

†† Nearly always, you need to *establish* lower cards that are not immediately tricks.

This is especially true when you are playing in no trump contracts:

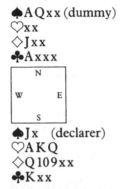

♠AQxx (dummy)  You are in 3NT and the heart jack
♡xx            is led. Count; you can only see six
♢Jxx           certain tricks. Your only chance of
♣Axxx          making nine tricks is to *establish*
               your diamond suit.

♠Jx   (declarer)
♡AKQ
♢Q109xx
♣Kxx

Take the first trick. Lead a diamond immediately and lose to the king. Win whatever is returned and lead another diamond, losing to the ace. Win any return. Now you have *established* three diamonds which, with one spade trick, three hearts and two clubs, add up to nine tricks – 3NT.

If you fiddle with any suit except diamonds, you will go down. Let us put in all four hands:

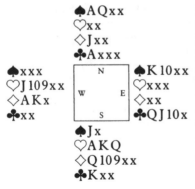

♠AQxx                    Suppose after the heart jack is led
♡xx                      that you play out the other top
♢Jxx                     hearts. Now you will have estab-
♣Axxx                    lished two heart tricks in a defen-
♠xxx   ♠K10xx            der's hand. The defence will also
♡J109xx ♡xxx             make at least the diamond AK and
♢AKx   ♢xx               the spade king, a total of five
♣xx    ♣QJ10x            tricks. You will be one down –
♠Jx                      because you *established their suit* for
♡AKQ                     them instead of *establishing* your
♢Q109xx                  own.
♣Kxx

When aiming to establish cards, remember you are playing two hands:

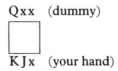

Qxx   (dummy)

KJx   (your hand)

Lead any of the honours from either hand and knock out the ace, and you have two tricks.

And you can establish a trick in this way:

xxx

AKxx

Play out the A K and then another, which loses. If the cards are 3–3 in the defenders' hands, the last x – the thirteenth card in the suit – will be a trick.

From these examples, it should be plain that contracts cannot be made by simply crashing out aces and kings. If you hold all the aces and kings, which you probably won't do in a lifetime of bridge, you may only make eight tricks.

So, at intervals during the play, you must surrender a trick with the object of making another later on.

This is anathema to most beginners, who invariably try to take all the tricks. Don't. Realistically, a declarer can afford to lose three tricks and make a contract of 4♡ or 4♠, four tricks and make 3NT – and this is roughly what happens in everyday bridge.

If you *can* take all the tricks, you should bid a grand slam. This you won't attempt until we introduce you to such dizzy heights in Chapter 7, and it is a rare occurrence anyway.

So, an early lesson to fix in your mind: don't be afraid to lose tricks,   †††
within reason. With a Q J 10 in your hand, your thinking should not be negative: 'I can't play this suit, I shall lose two tricks.' Certainly you will; the best player who ever lived cannot take an ace with a small card.

Think positively: 'I have a trick in this suit after the ace and king have been played.'

**Finessing**

Now for another way, a very common one, of making extra tricks. Some beginners pick up the principle of the finesse quickly, others take time. We shall linger on the subject.

A finesse may gain a trick when you hold divided honours:

AQ

xx

The ace is a certain trick, but if you next lead the queen it will lose to the king. But if you lead from the hand with the small cards *up to* the AQ and play the queen, you will take two tricks if the king is on your left, only one if it is on your right. Instead of taking only one trick, you have given yourself a fifty-fifty chance of taking two.

Be absolutely clear about finessing, by studying the following examples. The first is *not* a finesse:

KQ

xx

The king and the queen are cuddling together, as they should. When you lead the king, he will be taken by the enemy ace – but his sacrifice will not be in vain. The queen survives to take the next trick.

This *is* a finesse:

KJx

xxx

If the king sallies forth, he gets the treatment as before. His faithful valet, the jack, follows and perishes at the hands of the enemy queen. Both sacrifices are in vain. Neither has taken a trick.

Now try leading a small card *towards* the KJx and play the jack. You can't see where the ace and queen are, but favourably placed they will not be such a menace:

KJx

Qxx       Axx

xxx

Now the jack is chopped by the ace, but the king survives.

KJx

AQx ☐

xxx

Now again the jack survives. Later, when you regain the lead in your own hand and lead towards the remaining cards, the king also survives. You take finesses by leading *towards divided honours*. In the last case, both the king and the jack take tricks, nor can the opponents do anything about it. Had the second player put up a high card, the ace or the queen, the result would have been the same.

Of course, if the cards lie:

KJx

☐ AQx

xxx

you are simply unlucky. You lose both tricks but – and this is the whole point of the finesse – you lose nothing by trying.

A dictionary definition of a finesse is 'an adroit and delicate manoeuvre'. In bridge it is an attempt to take a trick with a lower card when a higher one is around. The attempt will succeed half the time and, however much adroitness is employed, fail half the time.

But without a finesse, you lose *all* the time. In betting language, by taking a finesse you are comparatively on the odds to nothing.

Another finesse situation: you frequently hold a trump suit like this:

AKJxx

xxx

If you play out the A K, you will probably lose the third round of the suit to the queen. If you lead from the small cards *up to* the A K J, and insert the jack, you have a 50–50 chance of finding the queen on the 'right' side, and losing no trick.

You often need to finesse against lower cards, too, for instance:

Q10xx

Kxxx

You are sure to lose the ace, but you try the finesse of the 10 to avoid also losing to the jack.

The next example, although slightly different, is the same in principle:

Axx

QJ10

If you lead out the ace, then the queen, you will lose a trick to the king. But if you lead the queen, the king will be caught in a sandwich if it is on your left. If it is played on the queen, put up the ace and make three tricks. If it is not played, 'run' the queen (play low from the other hand), and then do the same with the jack – still three tricks. Only if the king is on your right do you lose a trick.

This is the same sort of thing:

AQ109

Jxx

You *can* lead a little card and finesse the queen. However, if you are successful you will end up in the wrong hand to repeat the manoeuvre a second time. (Remember, you have to lead from the hand which takes the trick.)

†    Much better to lead the jack and, if the king does not appear on your left, run it (play a low card from the other hand). You are then correctly placed to take the finesse again.

This is the same principle:

Kx

xx

You cannot win by leading the king. If you lead *up to* the king, you win if the ace is on your left.

Be quite clear about finessing. If you don't finesse you are sure to lose a trick. If you do, you may gain an extra one. It is as if you were told that by crossing the road at one point you were sure to be killed, but at another you had an even-money chance of survival. There is no doubt which you would choose.

Convince yourself of the merits of finessing by putting down various combinations of divided honours, AQx, AJ10, KJx, etc., with some small cards facing them. Scatter the rest of the suit anywhere between the other two hands, and see for yourself how the finesse gains more than the feeble way of playing out the top cards first.

*Enjoinder*

Playing in a suit contract, it is best to draw out your opponents' trumps before playing any other suit (unless there is a reason not to, which will be explained later). If you do not draw trumps, the defenders will use theirs to trump your other high cards.

**Playing the hand, defenders**

Dummy goes down. In the pause while the declarer looks at it, you – now a defender – assess your chances of defeating the contract.

Remember this: you only need so many tricks to beat it. Four tricks won by the defence beats 4♡ or 4♠. Five tricks beats 3NT.

Don't worry about losing tricks. The declarer is going to make most †††
of them, whatever you do. There is no way you can take the aces and kings in declarer's and dummy's hands.

Your choices are:

● to take tricks, or prepare to take tricks – but only if you can with safety;

†††   • until you see a line of play – and this is just as important – *don't give unnecessary tricks away*. Wait for tricks to come to you.

†††   All defence is based on this: if you can't be aggressive, be safe.

A single example covers this precept. Remember the declarer's finesse position, like this:

KJx

xxx

Now add your possible cards:

KJx

   AQx (you)

xxx

If you lead out the ace and queen, you make one trick and declarer makes two. Two tricks given away for nothing. If you lead another suit, declarer is going to finesse towards your AQ at some stage – and will make no tricks – while *you* make two, or even three.

The difference between no tricks and two tricks is the difference between a contract made and a contract beaten. More than enough. Generally a single trick holds the balance.

If in doubt, play safe. Here is a routine hand to illustrate the point:

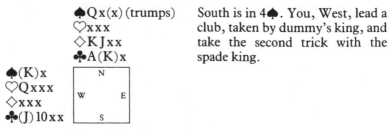

♠Qx(x) (trumps)        South is in 4♠. You, West, lead a
♡xxx                   club, taken by dummy's king, and
♢KJxx                  take the second trick with the
♣A(K)x                 spade king.

♠(K)x
♡Qxxx
♢xxx
♣(J)10xx

Leaving aside any other factors which may be present your next lead should be ... a club. Dummy, of course, has the top club, but declarer is going to make it anyway. Your club is the correct choice, *through strength* and not giving anything away.

††   To put it another way: as a defender, if you see no good line of

attack, try to lose to the tricks the declarer is sure to make. Don't help. Make declarer work for a living!

On lead as *East* you might also choose to lead a club, but you have another option. Look at dummy on your right; the weakness is in hearts. From the East position, a heart lead will be through the declarer's supposed strength up to your partner's possible high card and into dummy's weakness.

The very opposite of this, and a lead you will reject as absurd, is a diamond from East into dummy's strong K J. If your partner has the queen, it will be gobbled up immediately.

And here are two more general rules to follow, until you know when to break them:

*Second player plays low*    †††
As North you play your lowest card.

```
          Q73
x (led)  ┌─────┐  Axx
         │     │
         └─────┘
```

*Third player plays high*    †††

```
          Jxxx
x (led)  ┌─────┐  Kxx
         │     │
         └─────┘
```

You play the king. You don't think to yourself, 'I can't possibly. It will be taken by the ace.' It probably will be. But if you play a little 6, or something, declarer will take it with the 7 or an equally low card. So what are the odds? The odds in your favour are that your partner may hold the queen and, once your king is taken by declarer's ace, will take a trick in the suit later on.

Don't forget your partner!    †††

One other point about this: third player plays only as high a card as is needed:

```
          Q102
x (led)  ┌─────┐  KJx
         │     │
         └─────┘
```

Dummy plays the 2 and you put up the jack to force out the ace.    †

And just in case there is some confusion in your mind, these plays relate to the defenders. Declarer, with a view of twenty-six cards, can play high, low, middle or any old way.

We have not so far made defence sound very exciting (it is, you will find out). We are stressing caution because, if you think about it, that is exactly what defence is – defensive.

Try a comparison again with making a fruit pie for four people (a contract, say, of 4♡). As the opponents, you cannot expect to prevent a pie being made at all. A kitchen exists, and inside it a cooker; the ingredients are being purchased, and the two cooks are able. It is inconceivable that they cannot make some sort of pie – inconceivable that a declarer in 4♡ cannot make *any* tricks.

That is the cold light of reason. It follows that the object of the opponents will be the more realistic one of making the pie insufficient for four guests, or inedible.

Which means using guile. Your intention is not to blow up the kitchen with gelignite; you don't know where to buy gelignite, we hope. You need to be patient, conserving your strength and preparing to launch a counter-attack at a suitable time.

You might, for instance, arrange for the greengrocer to deliver a box of gooseberries, labelled 'Plums'. That would fool only the most moronic cook, but it would cause a set-back. You might telephone, at a crucial moment during the cooking, with a message that an aunt in Ireland is ill (having first discovered that the cook has an aunt in Ireland – slow, preparatory work) and then, while the cook is out of the kitchen, sneak in and remove three of the twenty-six plums, or switch the sugar and salt. That would be guileful, but to ring with news of a great-uncle in Ulan Bator would be fatuous; nobody who reads this book has a great-uncle in Ulan Bator. Your defence has to be governed by what is possible, and what is impossible.

There will, admittedly, be some occasions when nothing but all-out attack will prevail. Then you must muster your forces and invade the kitchen. But much more often you wait, and watch for opportunities to come to you, or (by no means impossible) for the cooks to make a mistake.

This is what defence is all about: patience, skill, judgement of when to make a forward move and collaboration between two partners.

## Opening leads

As a defender you begin with the opening lead. It is made blind, before dummy appears, and what you choose is very important.

The following table gives the correct card to lead from any combination of cards which you may hold. We know it is a lot to take in so early on; but don't skip it. Refer back to it again and again until you know the leads by heart. Sorry, this needs to be learned if you want to be a passable player. Thousands of bridge players get these leads wrong, with the result that their play in defence begins in confusion.

The correct card to lead is shown in heavy type in the examples; they are not in any particular order.

---

Top of sequence of three or more: **AKQ**, **KQJ**, **QJ10**, etc. down to **1098**.

Higher of any two cards: **J4**, **75**, etc.

'Top of nothing' (holding no honour): **975**, **763**, etc.

Lowest from an honour: Q**74**, J**53**, etc.

Fourth highest (fourth from the top) of a suit of four cards or more:

Q7**5**3, J86**4**2 but if the suit is headed by a sequence, **Q**J1073, lead the top.

The highest from K**Q**10, **Q**J9, J**10**8.

Top of two internal honours (against NTs): K**J**10, etc.

With two touching honours, **A**K753, **K**Q76, etc., lead the     † top against a suit contract, the **fourth** highest against NTs.

---

You may be wondering, 'Why should these leads be so important? For instance, if I have a sequence of QJ10 what's the difference between any one of the three? They are all of the same value.' True, it doesn't matter to *you*.

But you have a partner.

You are not trying to defeat the declarer single-handed. In defence, your partner is every bit as important as you are and, because neither of you can see the other's hand, the only way to concoct a plan of action is to exchange information by means of the cards you play.

The standard opening leads begin that vital exchange.

If you lead a queen you are guaranteeing to hold the jack, and perhaps the 10, underneath it. You are also, and this is equally important, denying the king in your hand; otherwise, from KQJ, the king would have been your lead. In the same way, the lead of a 2 promises to be the lowest card of four, to signal an honour above it, or to be a singleton.

In brief your opening lead tells your partner something useful. Lead the wrong card and you tell a lie.

††† And the other half of this story should easily spring to mind. When one partner leads a card *the other has to look at it to see what it means*. Alas! This is a blind spot and worth a whole bucketful of warning daggers.

The *choice* of a lead comes in a later section. For the moment, your first choice will be, if your partner has bid, a lead of that suit. Pick the correct card in it from the table above – and do not listen to anyone who tells you always to lead the highest card in your partner's suit. You don't.

The lead of the top of a sequence, say K Q J, is one of the best in the game. It is safe; and, after the ace has gone, should take one or two tricks.

*Against a suit contract*, other reasonable leads are: the top of two touching honours; a singleton (you may be able to trump – in bridge parlance to 'ruff' – when next the suit is led); a doubleton (a possible ruff on the third round); a long suit; and sometimes a trump.

††† The dreadful leads are from divided honours, A Q, K J, A J; they are almost guaranteed to give a trick away.

††† Equally abominable is the lead of an unsupported ace (an ace without the king underneath it) or a small card away from an ace. The object of aces is to take kings and queens, not the miserable little 2s and 3s which will be played if you lead them out. An ace led wildly is the equivalent of firing your ammunition into the air. And a king led without the queen underneath it is just as frightful.

††† In these cases, holding K J x, A Q x x, A J x x x, A x, A x x, A x x x, etc., *lead another suit*.

If you are still asking why, look at it like this:

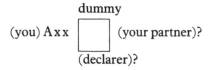

dummy

(you) A x x       (your partner)?

(declarer)?

Who is most likely to hold the king? Declarer is playing the contract and has the high cards, so you *imagine* the king in that hand until you know differently. That means that not only must you not lead your ace now, but you must also resist the temptation to lead it later.

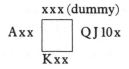

xxx (dummy)

Axx ☐ QJ10x

Kxx

Now you can see that declarer never makes a trick with the king, unless you lead the suit.

*Against a no-trump contract* your object is to *establish* the small cards in a suit. The fourth highest of your longest suit is standard (the reason will be explained why later). You lead your fourth highest from any combination, AJ863, A7542, KJ973, regardless of split honours. Your most urgent task is to set about your suit.

However, if your suit is headed by a sequence, for example ††
J10963, you lead the highest card.

Lastly, a RULE. You *lead* the top of a sequence, you *play* the bottom ††
one. If you are leading from QJ10, you lead the queen. If the suit is led by your partner, when it comes round to you you play the 10.

This helps your partner to identify your holding. Suppose:

xx (dummy)

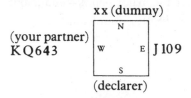

(your partner)
KQ643

J109

(declarer)

Your partner leads the 4, you put on the 9 and declarer takes the trick with the ace. Partner knows you have the J10 – declarer holding either of them would not have wasted the ace.

In the same way you *play* the lower of any two touching cards in the ††
pack. You are always denying holding the card underneath the one you play.

Now for a shorthand version of these pages:

*Declarer*

• Pause, look at and assess your hand and dummy's combined before you begin to play.

- When you can, draw the opponents' trumps before you do anything else.
- Make extra tricks by finessing.
- Playing in no trumps, establish your best (usually your longest) suit.

*Defenders*

- Yours is the most difficult part of bridge, so start right. Memorize the correct leads from every holding. You will meet people who have been playing for twenty, thirty or forty years who lead the wrong cards. Don't be among them.
- If you can't be aggressive, be safe. Let the declarer worry about taking tricks; most of yours will come to you during the play. And that means, once again, don't crash out unsupported aces. Wait, and play them on top of declarer's kings and queens. There is no *hurry* with aces. They'll still take tricks later in the play.
- Playing against no trumps, aim to establish a suit.

These pages have given you a good deal to think about on playing the cards. Don't worry. Try to remember the major points – and major faults – and refer back when you feel in need.

**State of play**

No change.

# 3  Bidding: the next stage

We have reached this point. The opener bids a suit. Partner either passes, supports the suit or responds in no trumps. Opener, in turn, bids higher or exercises the option to pass.

What messages they send to each other are entirely governed by the categories of points in Chapter 1.

Only one other alternative is possible. The responder may propose a different suit:

$$1\heartsuit - 1\spadesuit$$

The word that matters is 'propose'. As responder you are not saying, 'I can't bear your suit, we'll make mine trumps.' You are proposing an alternative.

And what happens when one party makes a proposal?

'Will you . . .?' he asks.
She adores him. 'Yes,' she breathes rapturously.

She can't stand the sight of him. 'Not on your life,' she replies curtly.

She is uncertain, because of his habit of scratching his behind. 'I don't know,' she says doubtfully, 'perhaps if you'd give up . . . well anyway, I'd like time to think it over.'

It would be an irritating maiden who just walked off without saying a word.

So here is the difference between responder's limit bid and a change of suit. The limit bid is a statement of fact, 'That is what I have. Leave it there or go on as you like.' But in changing the suit responder is putting forward a proposal. Common sense and common courtesy dictate that there should be a reply.

The option to pass no longer exists. Opener is forced to bid again.

*Responder*

When you suggest a new suit, because the opener is *forced* to bid, you need not jump to a limit. You will have an opportunity to bid again so you can make a simple response at the lowest level, inside the full range of 6–15pts.

(Opening 1♡):   You hold:  ♠K 10 x x
       ♡x x
       ♢A x x
       ♣x x x x  bid 1♠

   or this  ♠A J 10 x x
       ♡x x
       ♢A Q x
       ♣K x x  still bid 1♠

The first hand has 7pts and the second 14pts, but it doesn't matter. You can reveal your strength or weakness on the next round of bidding.

†  (Note that on the first hand you bid 1♠. It is – nearly – always right to bid a four-card heart or spade suit in preference to 1NT. And if you hold four hearts and four spades, bid hearts first. Also note that, when introducing a new suit, you do not count points for shortages.)

(Opening 1♡):   You hold:  ♠x x x
       ♡K x
       ♢Q x x
       ♣A Q x x x bid 2♣

Now your simple raise has to go up to the two level, and because of this you need more security – *at least 9pts and a five-card suit.*

It follows that with
    ♠x x x
    ♡x x
    ♢Q x x
    ♣A J x x x (7pts)

or with   ♠Jxx
          ♡xxx
          ◇Qxx
          ♣AQxx (no five-card suit)

you must bid 1NT, not 2♣.

*Opener's rebid*

With your lowest category of points, 13–14,
you can say no bid to your partner's *limit bid*.
To a *change of suit* you no longer can.
  So now, instead of passing:

with 13–16pts make a minimum rebid;
with 17–18pts bid up;
with 19–20pts bid the game.

And if responder changes the suit a second
time:

1♡ – 1♠
2♡ – 3♣

you must bid yet again.

*Responder*

But if the opener changes the suit *you* do not
have to bid again. You cannot be made to bid a
miserable 6pts more than once (except in
special circumstances which are explained
later).
  However, holding more than 10pts, you will
make another bid.

To summarize: the responder, when changing the suit, dispenses with
the three categories and makes a simple bid at the next level, to which
opener is forced to make a second bid. On the second round of
bidding, both opener and responder clarify their strengths or weaknesses.

And the bidding is kept low. When both partners are making suggestions, and having to raise the ante each time they make one, they need space to reach the best contract.

> I suggest gooseberries.  – What about plums?
> Gooseberries.  – Damsons, then?
> OK, damsons.  – Damson pie coming up.

$$1\diamondsuit - 1\heartsuit$$
$$2\diamondsuit - 2\spadesuit$$
$$3\spadesuit - 4\spadesuit$$

And finally it amounts to this: each partner communicates a proposition, and listens to the reply. You listen, consider what your partner has and see how it fits in with your hand. You do not stare at your own hand in a kind of idiotic isolation; you *listen* to your partner. Partnership bidding is an exchange of information, in order to find out:

- which suit should be trumps, or whether to play in no trumps;
- the combined number of points in the two hands, and how they fit together, and, from that, the level to which the bidding should go.

Now we need to put some flesh on the bones of the opener's rebid, after partner has changed the suit.

It looks formidable, but hold on tight to the simple logic behind it: if you open with minimum points, you will make a minimum rebid; if you are better, your rebid will be higher; and if your opening is in the top 19 or 20pts, you will bid the game. So:

Responder has made a limit bid.

Rebid as in Chapter 1, but if responder bids 1NT you may pass or bid **1** or **2** below from choice.

Responder has changed the suit.

*Opener with 13–16pts.* Bid a minimum.

**1** Rebid your suit, if you have five or more:

$$1\heartsuit - 1\spadesuit$$
$$2\heartsuit$$

2 Rebid a suit *lower* than the one you opened:

1♡ – 2♣
2◇

With a choice of these two, the second is a †††
much better bid, i.e. with:

♠xx           1♡ – 2♣
♡AQJxx        2◇ is much more
◇KJxx         illuminating than merely
♣Ax           repeating your suit.

3 Support your partner's suit, with four or
more:

1♡ – 1♠
2♠

4 With exactly 15 or 16pts and no singleton,
rebid 1NT over a one-level response:

1♡ – 1♠
1NT

Rebid 2NT over a two-level response:

1♡ – 2♣
2NT

*Opener with 16 or 17pts* has another option (see
page 58).

*Opener with 17 or 18pts.* Try for game.

1 Rebid your suit, an extra level higher, if it is
strong – at least a six-carder:

1♡ – 1♠
3♡

2 Support your partner's suit, an extra level
higher, with four or more:

1♡ – 1♠
3♠

**3** With exactly 17 or 18pts, and no singleton, rebid 2NT over a one-level response:

1♡ – 1♠
2NT

Rebid 3NT over a two-level response:

1♡ – 2♣
3NT

*Note.* You may only jump the bidding in your own or your partner's suit – not in a new suit (yet).

*Opener with 19 or 20pts.* Bid the game.

**1** Rebid your own suit, but it must be very strong:

1♡ – 1♠
4♡

**2** Support your partner's suit, with four or more:

1♡ – 1♠
4♠

**3** Rebid 3NT.

Note the precision of the opener's rebids in no trumps:

|  |  |
| --- | --- |
|  | Over a one-level response: |
| 1NT shows 15 or 16pts | |
| 2NT shows 17 or 18pts | |
| 3NT shows 19 or 20pts | |
|  | Over a two-level response: |
| 2NT shows 15 or 16pts | |
| 3NT shows 17 or 18pts | |

*Responder*

Holding less than 10pts you will not usually bid again. However,

1 if opener bids a second suit:

1♡ – 1♠
2♣

you have been given a choice. If you have more clubs than hearts, pass. If you have more hearts, or an equal number of both, correct the bid to 2♡. This is giving simple preference (but see Chapter 14).

**2** If opener makes a rebid other than minimum, showing 17 or 18pts (say 2NT), you must do some simple arithmetic. With 8pts or more, bid game.

All the bids on these pages are really based on common sense plus an ability to add up to 26. We know that none of it is very exciting, points are dull things, and in fact you will find out later that they are only one of the considerations in bidding. The distribution of the cards – the lengths and shortages of your suits – and whether you have a 'fit' with your partner are equally important, and should dictate the ultimate level of the later bidding.

Meanwhile, impress the point-counts on your mind, and you won't go far wrong.

'You' means you and your partner. Don't forget your partner. Glorious isolation will do you no good. We know that, at the beginning, you will concentrate fiercely on your own cards, and when your partner bids you will take it in with only half your mind. That may be understandable at first, but the inattention must not last long.

You can *see* the cards you hold. You have to *deduce* from the bidding †††
what cards are in your partner's hand, and relate them to your own. It is by exchanging messages and listening to each other that you explore the way to the best final contract.

Don't forget your partner. †††

You may think we are labouring the point, so why the daggers? You are quite capable of ringing a friend and agreeing to meet for luncheon at 1 o'clock – roger and out. Neither of you is going to arrive for tea at midnight. But the messages of bridge players, and not only beginners, are often so garbled in the transmission (or, worse still, ignored) that,

were they making a date, one would turn up for dinner on Sunday and
the other for breakfast on Tuesday week.

Beginners, in particular, tend to misinterpret their partner's bids,
like this:

> 1♡ – 1♠
> 2♡ (My partner doesn't like my suit.)

Not so. Dislikes don't come into it at this stage. The responder may
hold three nice hearts – not the four necessary to raise in hearts in the
first round – and is making a natural first reply of 1♠.

Now let's focus on the two obvious faults, overbidding and underbidding. Despite the tidiness and accuracy of the point-counts, there
is plenty of both around.

Overbidding is the less common among beginners, but it happens
among the brighter sparks: 'I'll risk 4♠,' meaning, 'I haven't got the
points but I like a gamble, so here goes.'

In their minds is the thought that partner, having shown 6–10pts, is
pretty well sure to have ten. Yet, if you think about it, there are five
possible numbers of points in partner's hand, 6, 7, 8, 9 and 10, so
there is only one chance in five that the maximum 10 will appear.

There are plenty of risks and gambles that should be taken in
bridge, but not when the odds are stacked against you like this. If you
went through life relying on one-in-five chances, you would end up in
the bankruptcy court, the madhouse or the grave.

Underbidding is much more common. Here is a real three-daggers'-worth in the early stages:

*Responder*

(Opening 1♡):    1♠ with ♠A K J x
                   ♡x x
                   ◇K J x
                   ♣Q x x x

(Rebid 2♡):     ???
There is a rhythm about

1♡ – 1♠
2♡ – 2NT

which is completely false in this case. Your bid is 3NT of course.

††† Opener's 13 and your 14 come to 27, a game call. *You* are the one who knows this. You must not leave it to your partner by making a puny, inaccurate bid of 2NT.

† Underbidding is the outstanding fault of inexperienced players. It isn't that they cannot count up to 26 – a child can do that – rather that they don't think of the content of their partner's hand.

We also discern a touch of modesty that precludes a leap straight to 3NT or 4♠, as though it were a brazen, unladylike or ungentlemanly piece of aggression. Forget it. Call a spade a spade; call your four spades four spades; and your three no trumps three no trumps.

Here is a résumé of the bidding:

---

*Opener*

Open one of a suit with 13–20pts.

*Responder*

With four trumps or more, support partner's suit:

at the two-level with 6–10pts;
at the three-level with 11–12pts;
at the four-level with 13–15pts.

Lacking another bid, reply in no trumps:

1NT with 6–10pts;
2NT with 10–12pts;
3NT with 13–15pts.

If changing the suit, make a minimum response
at the one-level with 6–15pts;
at the two-level with 9–15pts and five trumps.

*Opener's rebids*

| | | |
|---|---|---|
| With 13–16pts | i | *To all single-raise limit bids* |
| | | except 1NT – no bid; |
| | | to a 1NT response – no bid or |
| | | make a minimum rebid. |
| With 17–18pts | | make an encouraging rebid. |
| With 19–20pts | | bid game. |
| | ii | *To double-raise limit bids* |
| with 13–14pts | | no bid. |
| With 15pts plus | | bid game. |
| | iii | *To a change of suit, at the* |
| | | *one-level* |
| with 13–16pts | | make a minimum rebid. |
| With 17–18pts | | make an encouraging rebid. |
| With 19–20pts | | bid game. |
| | | *At the two-level* |
| with 13–15pts | | make a minimum rebid. |
| with 15–16 points | | make an encouraging rebid. |
| With 17pts plus | | bid game. |

*Responder's rebids*

With   6–10pts – no bid (but see previous page).
With 10–12pts – bid higher.
With 13–15pts – bid game.

---

It will not have escaped you that so far the bidding has been confined to one side, the other staying obligingly dumb. Of course bridge is not like that. Bidding is fiercely competitive, and we come to the cut-and-thrust in Chapter 5.

Meanwhile, the more certain you are about bidding between two partners, the more easily you will handle matters when the pace hots up.

We have assembled the ingredients for a pie. The two partners have agreed the fruit and the quantity, and therefore how many people it will serve – one, two, three or four. At this stage it is rather rough and ready, so we shall add some trimmings.

These take the form of notes and explanations. They are not absolutely necessary at this stage, but you should refer back to them as soon as possible, and absorb the points made.

### Trumps

As you have seen, eight trumps are needed to play comfortably in a suit contract. Nine are much better, but with seven your hand can be distinctly awkward – after all, the other side has nearly as many.

The eight-trump holding is guaranteed in the simple opening and response of 1♠–2♠, when each player promises at least four.

Other than this, if one player rebids a suit, showing at least five in it, the other now needs only three to support. Any three will do, however humble. So that:

> *Responder*
>
> Having enough points for a second bid, you †† can support partner's rebid of a suit with xxx.
>
> But two are not enough. Even a royal couple, K Q, if they have no entourage, will not suffice.

### Four- and five-card suits

You must have at least five in a suit to rebid it unaided. You must have a five-card suit for your first response at the two-level: 1♠–2♣. Otherwise four-card suits can be bid at will. For instance:

> 1♡ – 1♠
> 2♢ may have only four diamonds

> 1♡ – 1♠
> 2♡ – 3♣ may have only four clubs

**No trumps**

*Responder*

A bid of 1NT is a simple, all-purpose reply showing 6–10pts and nothing better to say. Sometimes your hand may look too feeble to mention, but even on a miserable 6pts you do not pass.

However, bids of 2NT and 3NT are quite different. The danger of playing in no trump contracts is always that the opposition will reel off a suit which you do not hold, so now you and your partner between you should guard all four suits. Constructive bidding between the two of you will reveal whether you do.

And if your opponents have entered the bidding (Chapter 5) you must hold one, preferably two, stoppers in their suit.

*Opener's rebid* (**1**)

Rebidding a suit higher than the one opened is called a reverse.

$$1\diamondsuit - 1\spadesuit$$
$$2\heartsuit$$

This cannot be a minimum bid, because partner – if weak and wanting to correct to the first suit – has *to go to the three-level*, in this case to $3\diamondsuit$.

So, to reverse, an opener needs at least 16pts and should also have five cards in the first suit bid.

In some cases the opener's reverse has to be at the three-level, and then the hand needs to be stronger still: 17pts at least or the equivalent in distribution, i.e.:

| | |
|---|---|
| ♠xx | $1\heartsuit - 2\diamondsuit$ |
| ♡AKJxx | 3♣ |
| ◇Ax | |
| ♣AJ10x | |

but take a couple of points away and all you can rebid is $2\heartsuit$. Equally:

♠xx  1♡–2◇
♡AKJxx  2♡
◇x
♣AJxxx

Many players overbid this hand, with 3♣.  ††
Don't be among them. To reverse you need at
least 16pts.

### Responder

Treat reverses as forcing and bid again, except
when your first response was 1NT.

### Opener's rebid (2)

If a player has first passed and then changed
the suit, the bid is not forcing:

    1 No bid  2 1♡
    3 2♣  4 ?

Partner need not (but may) bid again.

### Opener and responder

Do be quite clear that no bid is also a bid, one in the long run that you
make more than any other! Stop if you are not being forced and have
no more to say.
    You open 1♡ with:

♠x  and the bidding goes
♡AKJxx  1♡ – 1♠
◇AJxx  2◇ – 2♠
♣xxx

Perhaps you are thinking, 'What a partner! I have given a choice
between two suits and all I hear is a lot of nattering about another one.
I have only a singleton in it, so I'd better rescue into . . .'
    If you think like this you are in danger of blaming the messenger for
the message. Your partner heard you clearly but has no support for
your suits and probably a good six-card spade suit. Pass. If you bid
again you will only make matters worse.

## Some explanations

1 The reason why you open the bidding differently on four-card and five-card suits is to keep the bidding low while you are exploring.
   One example:

♠AQxx     You open the lower four-card suit, 1♣. If your partner
♡Kx        responds 1◇ or 1♡, you can rebid 1♠ – still at the
◇xxx       one-level. Had you opened 1♠ and partner responded
♣AQxx     2◇ or 2♡, you would have had to rebid 3♣ to show
           your second suit – two levels higher for the same result.

2 In the tables responder's points are duplicated: 6–10 and 10–12 because you can hold a 'good' or a 'poor' hand of 10pts.

   One measure of good and poor is the intermediate cards: 10s and 9s take tricks, 3s and 2s don't. K 10 9 8 is quite a decent suit and may take more than one trick. K 4 3 2 is a king heading a load of rubbish.

   More important is whether or not you have a good 'fit' with your partner's hand, and here shape and distribution begin to come into your calculations. For instance, you open 1♡ on this hand of 15pts:

♠AQxx     If your partner responds 1♠ you have a marvellous fit,
♡KJxxx    so you immediately upgrade your hand and bid 3♠.
◇Axx      But if your partner replies 2♣ you are temporarily
♣x         uninterested. Bid 2♡.

## Evaluating your hand

In Chapter 1 we said that responder could count points for shortages only when supporting partner's suit. That is on the first round of bidding.

On later rounds, either of the two can count a short suit as an asset, provided it is in the right place. For instance:

1♣ – 1♠
2♡ – 3♡
4♡

A singleton in either hand in the missing suit, diamonds, is worth two points.

This is just touching on the subject. You do not really keep on counting points for everything new that arises throughout the bidding. That would prove to be either too much of a straitjacket or might lead to your counting so many points that you went through the roof. You learn finally to think of length and shortages in the form of shape, and the fit between your hand and your partner's – but more of this later.

There is more detail in this chapter than you can be expected to absorb at once. But take heart! You now have an outline of simple bidding, excepting only opening bids in no trumps and bids on very strong hands.

In fact, Chapters 1 and 3 together constitute your reference book of straightforward bidding. Of course there are embellishments to come, but this is a solid foundation.

The point is that you can *learn* bidding. The play of the cards is another matter. We continue with it in the next section.

## State of play

After the deal, make sure that:

- one player has an opening bid in hearts or spades: maximum points, 19;
- responder's maximum points are 15;
- no one at the table has more than a six-card suit;
- only one partnership bids.

# 4 Play: the next stage

Inexperienced players nurse the delusion that bidding is the difficult part of bridge, and that whether or not a contract is made is a sort of act of God. This is absolutely the wrong way round. Most bidding, when you know the ground-rules, is easy. Playing the cards is much the greater challenge.

Liken bridge to planning a holiday. Margate, suggests one partner; Marbella, or possibly Monte Carlo, replies the other. Diamonds, spades or no trumps? A decision will usually be made without much difficulty.

But getting to your holiday destination – making your contract – is another matter. It *may* be easy, it may not. Skilled obstructionists are lurking in your way (striking air-traffic controllers or railwaymen); unexpected hazards (long fogbound delays, a tree across the line); your own carelessness (leaving the passports behind, running out of petrol). Acts of God (cyclones, earthquakes, plague) do not come into your considerations.

†† And so with playing the cards. Your opponents are there to obstruct you; you yourself may be careless, forgetting to draw all the trumps; hazards of all kinds are strewn across your path; bad luck may encompass you. Be prepared from the very start. Nothing in declarer play is more important than the moment when dummy goes down. That is when you pause and prepare yourself to play the hand.

Yet for most players that moment does not exist. They set straight off at a gallop, with only a hazy idea of what they intend to do. They play quickly to the first trick, then the second, then at some stage it dawns that the contract is going to fail.

Worse still, some play blindly right through to the end, then count their tricks and with oohs and aahs and crestfallen faces exclaim, 'One down, partner' (then, 'It couldn't be helped; the finesses were wrong/ the ceiling fell in,' or whatever springs to mind).

Bridge players do not behave like this in their ordinary lives – if they did, they would live in continual chaos. After all, you plan your journey to work, and check your watch to see that you are on time. Faced with a dinner party, you go down to the shops to buy the requisites. You don't wander aimlessly round the supermarket and

arrive home with twenty tins of cat food and a pomegranate. You plan.
And so you should with bridge. The cards are like the instruments
of an orchestra, with you as the conductor. You must understand
them, blend them together, conduct them with discipline and
rhythm, and harmony will result. So, as declarer, you make a plan at
the beginning of a hand, and keep a check during the play on how that
plan is going.

### Playing no-trump contracts

Almost always you will need to 'find' extra tricks to make your
contract. This means playing on your most promising suit, usually
your longest, and *establishing* small cards in it:

♠xxx            You are in 3NT, and a spade is led.
♡AJx
◇Axxxx
♣Qx

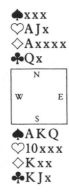

♠AKQ
♡10xxx
◇Kxx
♣KJx

Count your tricks. You have three spades, one heart and two
diamonds on top, and two clubs, once you have forced out the ace.
That is eight tricks; one short.

It is no use at all playing out your top cards, because you will run out
of steam at trick 8 and the defenders will take the rest. This is the same
as if the chap short of petrol in Chapter 1 decided to blind up the M1
with the wild hope that his fuel would last out. You, and he, would be
staking your future on impossibilities.

Your need is to establish your own small cards. Play out the ace of
diamonds, then the king, then a small one and lose it. If the cards fall
as is likely you will have *established* two little diamonds as tricks. Now
your haul is the original eight tricks, plus two diamonds – ten tricks.

This is the basis of all no-trump play. Go for your best suit, even if it   ††
means losing tricks on the way.

But there is another side to this, peculiar to no-trump hands. Before you begin to play you must ask yourself the reverse question: can the defenders establish their long suit before I can get at mine?

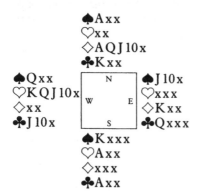

♠Axx
♡xx
♢AQJ10x
♣Kxx

♠Qxx
♡KQJ10x
♢xx
♣J10x

♠J10x
♡xxx
♢Kxx
♣Qxxx

♠Kxxx
♡Axx
♢xxx
♣Axx

You are in 3NT, and the *heart* king is led. (NB. In all hands in the book, South is the declarer.)

Count your tricks. You will be finessing the diamonds, but even if that goes wrong you have an easy nine tricks. But is there a danger? What about the lead of the *heart* king? Suppose you take it with your ace, and then lose a trick to the *diamond* king. The enemy will be able to run off four heart tricks which, with one diamond, puts you one down.

But if you *hold up* the *heart* ace the first time – play a little one, that is – and then again the second time, and take the third trick, by then East will have no hearts left after winning with the *diamond* king. No harm can now befall you. There will be more about holding up later. Meanwhile file this much as part of your plan.

### Playing in a suit

Now the trumps are the key to the hand. Yours will protect you against the opponents running off a suit; but they have trumps too which must be removed so that they cannot sneak in and take your other high cards.

So you begin the hand with the plan, 'I will draw (the opposition) trumps, unless there is a special reason not to.' Play yours out straight away, perhaps losing one on the way, until the other side have none left.

If you have eight trumps between your hand and dummy (as you should have) the likelihood is that the opponents' will fall 3-2. They will be exhausted in three rounds, leaving you two over. Of course they may not fall 3-2. You may be unlucky and find a 4-1 break against you, even a fearfully unlucky 5-0. You will only find out if you count the trumps as they are played.

The easiest way is to add up as you go along, like this: 'Four went on the first round, three on the second; that is seven gone.' If you now have five in the two hands, there is one left to draw.

You must get used to counting the trump suit (and, as soon as you can, the other suits). You neither want to draw too few – leaving one behind to ruff one of your high cards – nor too many, which may leave you so short of trumps that you lose control of the hand.

Now here are three standard ways of making a suit contract.

1 By taking finesses (noted in Chapter 2). If that's all there is to it, take them, cross your fingers and hope they are right.
2 By establishing a side suit, other than trumps (and usually in dummy) on which you can throw losing cards:

♠ Qxxx        You are in 4♠, and a club is led.
♡ QJ 10x
◇ xxx
♣ Ax

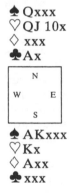

♠ AKxxx
♡ Kx
◇ Axx
♣ xxx

Count your losers: they are one heart, two diamonds and a club – one too many.

Now first draw trumps, until the enemy has none left. Then lead the *heart* king and *lose it to the ace.*

*Never be afraid of losing a trick in order to make more tricks.*    †††

In the hand above, the opponents will probably next make a club trick, then lead a diamond, which you take. After that you can play a small heart to the queen, and then discard two diamonds on your established hearts. Result: eleven tricks.

And note here: you first lead the *heart* king, the high honour from    †
the hand with the fewest cards. If you play the queen first and the ace takes it, on the next round of the suit you will be stuck in the

wrong hand. Always do this: for instance with K Q x facing A J x x x, lead out the K Q so as to end up where the length is.

In these first two ways of playing suit contracts you draw trumps first. In the third you won't. Your plan is to leave them until later.

**3** By ruffing in dummy:

♠xxx
♡x
♢xxxx
♣AJxxx

You are in an optimistic 4♠, and a diamond is led.

♠AKQxx
♡Axx
♢Axx
♣xx

Count your tricks. You have five spades and three aces – two short of 4♠. If you draw trumps that will be the result.

You don't. You first lead the *heart* ace, then ruff a heart in dummy. Play back to your hand with a spade, and ruff another heart in dummy. So two little trumps, which would have disappeared had you drawn trumps first, have made two extra tricks.

Often when ruffing in dummy you lose a trick first, but don't worry:

♠xxx
♡xx

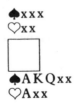

♠AKQxx
♡Axx

Play out the *heart* ace, then a small one which you lose (but would lose anyway); later ruff the third heart in dummy.

†††    Ruffing in dummy is all profit: but note, there is no advantage in doing the opposite – ruffing dummy's losers in your own hand. This foxes beginners at first, but you will understand if you think how the cards fall. Example, showing two suits:

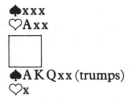

♠xxx
♡Axx

♠AKQxx (trumps)
♡x

Think. If you draw trumps and they fall in three rounds, the position will be this:

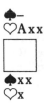

♠–
♡Axx

♠xx
♡x

The two trumps left in your hand are the absolute masters of the hand. You will make no extra tricks by ruffing dummy's losers with them.

ENTRIES

Remember, you always have to lead from the hand which took the last trick – your own or dummy's. Perhaps your plan is later to lead from one hand or the other to take a finesse or make some other play. For this to be possible you must have an entry, a high card, to get to that hand. If you aren't careful there won't be one.

Look at this hand:

♠xxx
♡Ax
◇J10xx
♣Qxxx

♠AKxxx
♡Kx
◇AQxx
♣xx

You are in 4♠ and a heart is led. Your certain losers are a trump and two clubs.

The contract depends on a successful diamond finesse, which means leading from dummy. But you cannot risk playing two or three diamonds straightaway, for at some stage they will be trumped. Your first priority is to draw trumps.

If you take the original heart lead carelessly with the ace, you will have knocked out your only entry to dummy to take the diamond finesse later. So you don't; you take it in your hand with the king.

And that was the very first trick of the hand. Play too quickly and you are down. Think and plan first, and you are home.

### Note about odds

With eight cards in a suit in two hands: A K J x x  x x x, the odds favour the queen being guarded, Q x x – take the finesse. With nine cards: A K J x x x  x x x, the chances are the queen will fall in two rounds – play out the A K.

### Summary of declarer play

Pause; look at the two hands clearly and as a whole; count your winners; count your losers; consider the dangers to your contract; form a plan.

#### MORE ABOUT THE DEFENCE

Now we are in the most difficult area of bridge, for declarer begins each hand with all the advantages. Think of it as a battle, and you'll see why.

Declarer general has all the troops in his hand and in dummy under unified command. He knows their strengths and their weaknesses, and can dispose them in any way he pleases.

Defender general? The defence does not have a general. It has two colonels commanding separate battalions. Neither knows what troops the other has, nor where they are.

In such circumstances in battle, the two battalions could fight separately, and outnumbered die glorious deaths. That is what thousands upon thousands of bridge players do. As defenders, they play their cards in a vacuum, ignoring their partners, squandering their resources and meeting defeat with a rueful, 'It couldn't be helped, partner.' It could, of course.

In real life what our two colonels would do would be to exchange information by way of signals, in order to fuse their forces and plan a joint strategy. And that is your object in defence. You signal to your partner by the way you play your cards.

The first signal is the opening lead. If you have memorized the opening leads in Chapter 2, you will know that if partner leads a king that is a signal that the queen, and perhaps the jack, is underneath it. The lead of a 9 will deny holding an honour – it will be the higher of two cards or the 'top of nothing'. And so on.

Now we come to the next stage of signalling. When your partner leads, you throw the highest card you can afford to ask for the suit to be continued; your lowest to show you are not interested.

Suppose that against a suit contract your partner leads an ace; certainly the king is underneath it, and you hold Qxx:

A (K and some others)    Q83

You throw the 8 to say, 'Carry on, I like it.' And exactly the same with:

83

In each case you can take the third round of the suit; in the first with the queen, in the second with a ruff. Conversely, with:

983

you throw the 3: 'I'm not interested.'

In the same way you throw high–low (a peter) to encourage – from Q432 the 4 followed by the 3 – and upwards, from 432 the 2 first, to discourage.

You also signal during the course of the play. If you have run out of a suit and have to discard, you throw a high card in the suit you would like led, A954. If you cannot afford one, holding say AKJ, throw a low one in another suit.

And do not pussyfoot with signals. Throw the highest card you can afford. Holding KQJ10, throw the king.

A very important injunction, worth twenty daggers if we allowed †††
them. *Signalling is only half of communication. The other half is partner looking at the cards played and reading their messages.*

What use is it if your partner makes impeccable signals, and you don't bother to look at them? Think of a doubles in tennis. You don't tear about the court trying to take every shot, leaving your partner a mere spectator. If you did, you would certainly be beaten, and equally certainly would not be invited to play with the same partner again. Bridge is no different. When you play the cards in defence, you call the shots and react in turn to each other's signals and play. As far as you can, you blend your partner's cards with your own and jointly put together a plan of action.

## Covering honours

This is the principal exception to the rule that second player plays low. Look at one suit in four hands:

$$A J x$$

$$K x x x \quad \boxed{\phantom{xx}} \quad 109 x$$

$$Q x x$$

The queen is led by declarer, and you are in second position. If you play low declarer will run the queen (play low from dummy), next finesse the jack, and make three tricks in the suit.

So you cover the queen with the king. Beginners can scarcely bear sending their king to perdition in this way, but see what happens. The ace takes the first trick, the jack the second, and your partner's 10 the third. And if your partner doesn't hold the 10 – nothing is lost.

The purpose of covering an honour with an honour is to set up a trick later on for your side.

Sometimes you do not cover honours, for instance:

$$Q J 109 x \text{ (dummy) } Q \text{ led}$$

$$\boxed{\phantom{xx}} \quad K x x$$

There is no prospect here of a trick for your side, so play low. Declarer just might have A x, leaving your king high after two rounds.

Equally, don't cover:

$$A x$$

$$K x x \quad \boxed{\phantom{xx}}$$

$$Q \text{ (led)}$$

Your king will be high after two rounds.

Covering honours is quite a complicated subject. A general rule is: when in doubt, cover; when it would be futile to do so, don't.

## Defending against no-trump contracts

Now your objective is not to take tricks quickly, but to establish a suit. This, of course, is declarer's object too, and often it can be a race between the two sides.

You cannot be sure which is the best suit to establish between you and your partner. The best try you can make is to lead your longest, choosing the fourth highest. (The reason for the fourth highest – fourth from the top – is explained in Chapter 8.)

And your lead in no trumps is quite different from that against a suit contract. You can lead away from aces, A x x x x; from divided honours, K J x x x; from touching honours, K Q x x x. (But if your long suit is one bid by the other side, ignore it and choose something else.) Except from a sequence of three, K Q J, Q J 10 etc., or from K Q 10 or Q J 9, you lead low.

One example should show the reason. South is in 3NT:

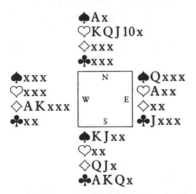

```
              ♠Ax
              ♡KQJ10x
              ◇xxx
              ♣xxx
♠xxx        ┌─────────┐   ♠Qxxx
♡xxx        │ N       │   ♡Axx
◇AKxxx      │W       E│   ◇xx
♣xx         │    S    │   ♣Jxxx
            └─────────┘
              ♠KJxx
              ♡xx
              ◇QJx
              ♣AKQx
```

If you lead out the diamond A K and lose the third round to declarer's queen, your partner, when taking a trick with the *heart* ace, will have no diamonds left to lead back to you. If you lead low, your fourth highest, you will lose the first trick and your partner still has a diamond to return.

And, in all ordinary circumstances, your partner *should* return your suit when getting in. There must be a very, very good reason not to, and more partnerships have dissolved in acrimonious bickering through this one failing than any other.

## Discarding

When discarding – throwing away cards when you cannot follow suit – you will first of all try to keep any honours you have guarded, Kx, Qxx, Jxxx. If you throw any of the small cards in these combinations, your honour could crash underneath declarer's higher honour.

Other important holdings are A 10 x x, K 10 x x, Q 10 x x. They may be worth two tricks if all the cards are retained. And 10 x x x or even 10 x x may surprise you by taking a trick. Don't scupper your defence by careless discarding.

## Defence in general

Beginners at defence often exclaim, 'I can't play that. They'll take it.' This is missing the point altogether. Of course the declarer is going to take most of the tricks. In defence you need four tricks to beat 4♡ or 4♠, and five to beat 3NT. You need to be patient, burrowing away during the hand and seizing opportunities when they come. Most often this means playing passively, not giving anything away, and waiting for tricks to come to you.

We know that in the early stages beginners find this the most difficult part of bridge. They cannot resist leading out their aces and other high cards.

Yet you must be patient.

Think of it from the opposite viewpoint. Cook's efforts to make a pie are being hampered by the fact that there appears to be a shortage of plums, and the sugar seems to have gone walkabout.

As an opponent it is not up to you to proffer extra plums or to locate the sugar.

So, for instance, you lead a card which you know the declarer is going to ruff (another play which beginners abhor), but by doing so you leave the declarer in the same unhappy position as before. You don't play out your lone ace until it is the trick which breaks the contract.

It is only when you see that declarer is sure to succeed, perhaps because there is a good suit in dummy on which to discard losers, that you switch from passive to aggressive. Now, in your hurry to take tricks, you take chances.

By now you must be saying, 'What a lot there is to remember!' Well, yes. But be encouraged by this: Chapters 1–4 in this book contain the basis of all simple bidding between two partners, and the play of the cards.

And although there may be a lot to remember, you need only remember one thing at a time. In the small, still moment when you are deciding whether to play an 8 or a 3, that is the only call on your memory. You are not pondering whether you should have bid four hearts, whether the cat is going to have kittens, or what the weather is like on Miami Beach. You are choosing between an 8 and a 3. And, put like that, it is not too difficult.

## State of play

No change. But now make sure you know how to cut for partners, who deals and who shuffles. It is explained at the end of the intro-duction.

# 5   Opponents join in the bidding

We have laid most stress so far on the counting of points as an accurate guide to bidding. On many hands that is all you need do:

  1♠ – 3♠
  4♠

should have at least eight trumps and about 26pts, and, with average luck, ten tricks should be made in the play. But there is more to it than than that – you may not have average luck!

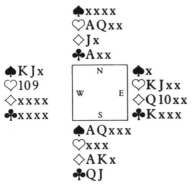

  ♠xxxx
  ♡AQxx
  ◇Jx
  ♣Axx

♠KJx
♡109
◇xxxx
♣xxxx

♠x
♡KJxx
◇Q10xx
♣Kxxx

  ♠AQxxx
  ♡xxx
  ◇AKx
  ♣QJ

You are playing in 4♠ and the *heart* 10 is led. You have nine trumps and 27pts, but the contract is· hopeless. As the cards lie you will lose two spades, two hearts and a club – two down.

The gremlins got at this hand. Three finesses out of three were wrong. You can only shrug it off as bad luck, but not before absorbing the next important lesson. *Points guide you in the bidding, but it is tricks which count in the play.* Here is another hand, similar to the one above except that your trump suit has been altered, and two little cards moved around. You still have nine trumps and 27pts:

♠xxx
♡AQxx
◇Jx
♣Axxx

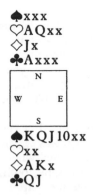

♠KQJ10xx
♡xx
◇AKx
♣QJ

Same number of points and trumps, but all you can lose is one spade, one heart and one club. You make ten tricks however the cards lie.

To some extent your bidding already takes account of distribution. Opener is counting extra points for length, and responder for shortages. Broadly speaking, if you bid your points they will translate into the right number of tricks. 'Broadly speaking' embraces the luck element. You win some, you lose a few, and that is the run of the game.

Later you will see more clearly how to combine points and distribution in your bidding, although already your instinct should be a good guide. Intuitively you probably appreciate that the second of the declarer's hands above, with its distribution and trump strength, is much more promising than the first, and that if you picked it up you would need no more than a nudge and a wink to bid game.

We accentuate trump strength and attractive distribution at this point because they are fundamental to the subject of this chapter – overcalling; that is, joining in the bidding after your opponents have called.

For now the scene has changed dramatically. No longer is one partnership exchanging bids in undisturbed tranquillity. Both sides are in the action. You are pitting your strength against their strength, and if you get it wrong you may suffer a humiliating and expensive penalty. Common sense is what you need. Rely on luck, and you may discover to your cost what a fickle friend she is.

The full scoring in bridge appears at the end of this chapter. For the moment we extract from it the penalties for going down, by looking at a hypothetical scoresheet:

| We | They |
| --- | --- |
| 500 | 1100 |
| 120 | |
| | 100 |
| 120 | |
| 740 | 1200 |
| (difference 460 to the other side) | |

The scores below the line are the three games won, two by you and one by your opponents. The 500 is your bonus for winning the rubber.

And the 1100? That is when you promised something you couldn't deliver, your opponents knew you couldn't, and doubled you.

Yes, you won the rubber – but you paid out on points. The penalty was a mighty one because you were 'vulnerable' when you went down. When a rubber begins, both sides are described as 'non-vulnerable'. After winning a game you become 'vulnerable' and the penalties increase sharply.

The penalties for failing to make a contract are as follows: for each trick you go down

| *Non-vulnerable* | *Vulnerable* |
| --- | --- |
| 50 | 100 |

Not much yet, but if your opponents *know* you have bid too high they will double you. A double is an overcall like any other, and it says, 'You can't make it. We'll have a bigger penalty, thank you.'

| | *Non-vul.* | *Vul.* |
| --- | --- | --- |
| For the first trick down, doubled | 100 | 200 |
| For second and third tricks down, doubled, each | 200 | 300 |
| For each additional undertrick | 300 | 300 |

††† That sort of trouble you can do without. The way to avoid it when overcalling is to *count your tricks, rather than your points.*

Here are two examples. In each case the player on your right has opened 1♠, and you are next to bid:

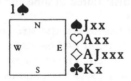

You have 14pts, but if you call 2♦ how many *tricks* can you guarantee? Suppose your partner has nothing and your left-hand opponent holds:

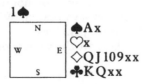

You will be doubled for penalties, and may make only two aces and a trump, three tricks – five down.

On such a hand you pass.                                                  †††
  But:

Again you have 14pts, but now you can guarantee six tricks: four trumps, an ace, and one with the KQ. You have trump strength and distribution on your side.

It doesn't matter what the next hand holds. You cannot be prevented from taking six tricks.

On this hand you bid 2♦.                                                  †††

An overcall is quite different from an opening bid. You open when no other player has shown strength. With luck you can reasonably expect the rest of the points to be fairly distributed among the other three hands – one of them your partner's.

You overcall after an opponent has shown the strength to open. Now the rest of the points can only be in two hands, and if luck is against you they will mostly be on your left. Then the next bid will be a double, and you can get ready with the sackcloth and ashes. It is no excuse to wail, 'Oh, but I had 13pts.' Maybe, but you didn't have the tricks.

So an overcall requires security, and the best security is a sound trump suit. For instance, J109xxx is much sounder than AKxxx. AJ1098 is fair; AJ432 is just waiting to be torn to pieces. In overcalling the emphasis is on tricks rather than points, and trumps matter most of all.

†††    And it follows that you *never overcall a four-card suit at the two-level* – and not often at the one-level (an alternative course of action appears later in this chapter).

It is the overcalls at the two-level which lead to the most painful doubles in bridge. At the one-level: 1♡ – 1♠, the danger is considerably less, although even this humble bid may not be safe.

Vulnerability is the factor to take into account. If you are not vulnerable and the opponents have a choice of doubling you or bidding on to game, they will nearly always bid on. When you are vulnerable they may choose to double for penalties.

With some provisos yet to come, here are the values you need to be able to overcall in a suit:

| | *Non-vulnerable* | *Vulnerable* |
|---|---|---|
| Overcall at one-level: | unimportant | 3½–4 tricks |
| two-level: | 5 tricks | 5½–6 tricks |

Now two more overcalls.

1 If you are really good you must say so by introducing your suit with
a jump:

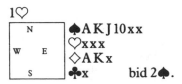

♠AKJ10xx
♡xxx
◇AKx
♣x        bid 2♠.

This is not a forcing bid but indicates that partner should support on
less than if the overcall had been a simple 1♠.

2 An overcall of 1NT is strong, showing 15–18pts and a balanced
hand.

And a possibly superfluous note. Do not in any circumstances overcall
the same suit as an opponent has opened, even with five or six of it.
Overcalls are often dicey; this one, when you *know* an opponent is
strong in your trump suit, would be bizarre. It is one thing to have the
misfortune to skid off the road, quite another to accelerate
deliberately into a tree.

As for the partners of the opener and overcaller, they should try to bid
normally:

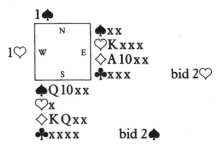

However, if you cannot make a normal bid you may have to pass:

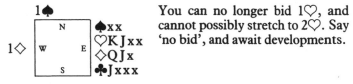

You can no longer bid 1♡, and
cannot possibly stretch to 2♡. Say
'no bid', and await developments.

Now consider the hand below. We have only your interests at heart when we insist that you pass in the East position. Nonetheless, even if our insistence were to be accompanied by massed trumpets, *some* players are still going to bid 2◇:

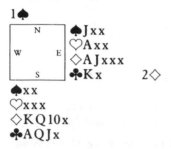

1♠

♠Jxx
♡Axx
◇AJxxx
♣Kx          2◇

♠xx
♡xxx
◇KQ10x
♣AQJx

If you are South and 2◇ is bid on your right, don't make the mistake of most beginners and bid 2NT. You have heard the sound of angel voices proclaiming that Christmas is coming.

††     Double, and enjoy the plum pudding.

A double is a bid which says to an opponent, 'You have no chance of making your contract. I'll make you suffer.' You have to double somebody's bid; to double a no bid would be as meaningless as a boxer claiming to win a fight without an opponent.

You use the single word 'Double' without frills – not 'I double you', or 'Double two hearts'; not with doubt in your voice, and certainly not with gloating in your manner.

A double, of course, gives notice to everybody at the table that you expect to beat the contract, so now we will look at the effect of it on the other two players.

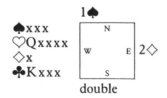

1♠

♠xxx
♡Qxxxx
◇x
♣Kxxx

2◇

double

West will plainly be dispirited at the turn of events, but there is nothing to be done. To rescue into 2♡ is not heroic but just stupid. Partner has chosen diamonds as trumps and partner, however suspect, must be trusted. What usually happens if you do bid 2♡ is that that 2♡ is doubled too. East turns up with a singleton heart and bids 3♢, and the contract escalates from the dangerous to the diabolical.

West must not even contemplate removing partner's bid with less than a strong six-card suit, say KQ109xx.

Now for North, who opened 1♠. North can see no reason why the contract of 2♢ should be beaten, but to retreat into 2♠ is a sin almost as heinous as that of West bidding 2♡. It is tantamount to saying, 'I heard your double, partner, but you are a liar and I don't trust you.'

So West and North pass and justice is done. East, who made the 2♢ bid, has sown the wind and must now reap the whirlwind.


### The takeout double

There will be more about doubling in a later chapter. For the meantime, remember that penalty doubles at this low level are made *after partner has bid*. They are equivalent to a response. The doubler takes into account partner's opening bid before stepping in with the big stick.

However, although a double is a bid like any other, it has two distinct meanings, according to how it is used. As the *first bid of a partnership*, other than a no bid, it carries a quite different message:

1♡

☐ double

*or*

no bid

☐ 1♡

double

This is a conventional bid with the meaning, 'I have a fair or good hand, but I don't know which suit should be trumps. Bid your best suit.'

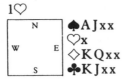

It would be preposterous to bid 1♠, naming spades as trumps, and find your partner with five diamonds and a singleton spade. You make a *takeout double*, rather a woolly description because it is in fact an order. It says, 'Partner, name your longest suit and I promise you support for it.' Partner *must* bid, even on the most pathetic, pointless hand. It is one of the deadly sins in bridge to pass a takeout double.

You cannot muddle the two doubles:

cannot be an order to bid because partner has already called 1♡. It is for penalties.

is the first bid of your partnership, and is a takeout double.

Don't worry too much about points. You should have roughly the values for an opening bid, but 11pts will be enough on some occasions. You need fewer, for instance, with good distribution, non-vulnerable 4-1-4-4 as above, or better still 4-0-5-4.

††     The takeout double is a very useful bid much under-used by inexperienced players, usually because they forget it. Don't make the same mistake. Use it every time, rather than naming a poor suit, provided you have some support for anything partner may reply:

1♡

 ♠Kxx
♡xx
◇KJxxx
♣AKx          Double, don't bid 2◇.

Your partner must respond with a suit, unless the next player bids:

1♡

double

2♡

Now West may pass because the doubler has another chance to bid.

Our fruit pie is now an unknown quantity. We don't know which of the two sides is going to make it. Opener has suggested one ingredient, say pears, and the doubler has promised to back plums, damsons or apples when partner names one of them. Who is finally going to gain the contract is still in the balance.

Opener has at least 13pts and doubler anything from 11 upwards. It is up to the other two hands to express their strength or weakness, and each has a way of doing so.

First the partner of the doubler:

double

1♡ 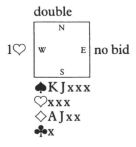 no bid

♠KJxxx
♡xxx
◇AJxx
♣x

After the opening 1♡ and the double, East and South have probably only about 10–14pts between them. As South you must differentiate between a bad hand, on which you would be forced to bid 1♠, and one like this with 9pts (or fewer points if you have strong distributional values). You show it by bidding 2♠.                    ††

Doubler, hearing your bid, may pass if minimum, or go on if the double was a strong one.

This accounts for three of the four hands. Now for the last one, the partner of the opening bidder, and this is a little more complicated. It is here to complete the pattern, but if you wish you may leave it for the time being.

double

1♡ [   ] ?

East can make a simple bid of 2♡, 1♠, 1NT or whatever, but this will show weakness. The way for East to show 9pts or more is again conventional:

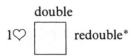

double

1♡ [   ] redouble*

South, who cannot hold anything, passes. Opening bidder also passes – waiting to hear what partner has to say before rebidding – and now the doubler is in a trap. What looked like a fair hand suddenly seems a potential disaster. 1♡ redoubled is 120, a game, and any overtricks score at 200 or 400 each according to vulnerability. A bid of some kind has to be found.

Suppose it to be 1♠. The redoubler holding, say:

♠K J 10 x
♡x x
◇A J x
♣J x x x

will immediately double for penalties – there are far too many guns here for 1♠ to be made by the other side.

With a different sort of hand, say:

♠Q x
♡x x
◇A K J x x
♣x x x x

the redoubler calls a suit, in this case 2◇.

So you can see that the seemingly unnatural redouble carries the meaning: I have at least 9pts; and leave the next bid to me because I may be able to double for penalties.

---

*A conventional bid in this instance. For a normal redouble see page 117.

This section on overcalling has run a fair distance. These are the most important parts to remember:

1 Do overcall when you can with safety.
2 Don't overcall at the two-level without a good suit.
3 Double for takeout whenever you can, but remember that you are forcing your partner to bid. After he has done so, only go on bidding if you have a good fit with partner's suit and an above-average hand.

We have put in rather a lot of 'don'ts', but with the intention that you should be wary, rather than timid. You want to get into the action whenever you can, and particularly when your opponents have a part score and, say, 2♡ gives them game. If you can give them a push, do so. They may be able to make 2♡ but not 3♡. Even at this stage, however, don't make dangerously silly overcalls. Weigh the risks against the benefits.

*And don't think it is a disgrace to go down.* Silly bids which attract great penalties to no purpose are one thing; competitive bids which cost you a few points and stop your opponents from making a game or part score are quite another. These can produce an invisible profit, not a loss.

If you watch experts playing rubber bridge you will see their scoresheets peppered with 50s, 100s and 200s above the line. They are not ashamed of them; nor should you be. Provided you play the cards correctly, each small penalty given away to save an opposition score is a Dunkirk-style victory. Temporarily defeated, you hope later to be rearmed with a game-going hand and counter-attack to good effect.

The best advice about overcalling belongs to the idiot boy's dream. Be bold, be cautious and be lucky at the same time. At any rate, be sensible.

### State of play

After the deal make sure that:

• opener's longest suit is hearts or spades: maximum points, 19;
• responder has a maximum of 15pts;
• neither has more than a six-card suit, *but* both sides can join in the bidding.

And now begin to score as you play.

SCORING

## Below the line:

Whatever you bid and make:

| | |
|---|---|
| spades and hearts | 30 a trick |
| diamonds and clubs | 20 a trick |
| no trumps | 40 first trick, 30 subsequent ones |

## Above the line:

Everything else, including overtricks:

| | |
|---|---|
| spades, hearts and no trumps | 30 pts a trick |
| diamonds and clubs | 20 pts a trick |

Penalties for failing to make a contract:

| | Non-vulnerable | | |
|---|---|---|---|
| | UNDBL | DBL | REDBL |
| First undertrick | 50 | 100 | 200 |
| For second and third undertrick | 50 | 200 | 400 |
| For each additional undertrick | 50 | 300 | 600 |
| | Vulnerable | | |
| | UNDBL | DBL | REDBL |
| First undertrick | 100 | 200 | 400 |
| For each additional undertrick | 100 | 300 | 600 |

For making a contract doubled with overtricks:

| | Non-vulnerable | Vulnerable |
|---|---|---|
| overtricks: | 100pts a trick | 200pts a trick |
| redoubled: | 200pts a trick | 400pts a trick |

Plus 50 points for making a doubled contract, or 100 points for making a redoubled contract

Other above-the-line scores:

| | |
|---|---|
| 'a hundred honours': four honours in the trump suit in any one hand at the table | 100 |
| 'a hundred and fifty honours': five honours in the trump suit | 150 |
| 'a hundred and fifty aces': all four aces in one hand in a contract of no trumps | 150 |

## Slams

| | *Non-vul.* | *Vul.* |
|---|---|---|
| Small slam: 6 of a suit or 6NTs bid and made | 500 | 750 |
| Grand slam: 7 of a suit or 7NTs bid and made | 1000 | 1500 |

| | |
|---|---|
| Rubber: in straight games | 700 |
| best of three | 500 |

## Incomplete rubber

If only one game has been completed, the winners of that game gain 300 points; if only one side has a part-score in a game not completed, that side gains 100 points.

# 6 No trumps come into their own

In the hurly-burly of the last chapter, both sides were sending out their troops of apples, pears, plums and so on in an attempt to outdo the other. There will have been successes and failures – and some casualties – in the competition to make a pie.

But in all this infighting one weapon has been an absentee. No one has yet *opened* with the straightforward proposal to make a mixed fruit pie.

So now we come to the bid which is at the very heart of your system; the opening 1NT. It completes the outline of simple bidding, excepting only the big stuff on very strong hands and the merry skirmishes on freakish ones.

The weak 1NT is an excellent opening bid, made on 12–14pts and a balanced hand. Its special merit is that, because it is the highest in the range of one-bids, if the other side want to bid they must do so at the two-level. An opponent who can bid a peaceful 1♡ over your 1♣ may find it unrealistic, if not impossible or hopelessly imprudent, to bid 2♡ over 1NT.

So a simple 1NT opening can be passed all round and win the day, even if the other side holds the majority of points. In that case it will probably go one or two down, but don't worry about that. It is better to lose 50 or 100pts above the line rather than, say, 60pts (the 2♡ the opposition could have made) below the line. If that is the outcome, the opening 1NT will have served its purpose.

That is, anyway, a negative view. 1NT may be made, or partner may raise it successfully to 2NT or 3NT.

We can deal with the opening 1NT briefly because the sequence of bids which follows it depends expressly on counting points. Almost all you need to do is add.

*Opener*

Open 1NT on 12–14pts, but never when holding a singleton.

> *Responder*
>
> With a good 11 or 12pts and a balanced hand
> bid 2NT. With 13pts plus and a balanced hand
> bid 3NT.

If responder raises to 2NT, only bid 3NT
when holding 14pts, or a good 13, otherwise
pass.

> With a good 11pts or more and a five-card
> major suit, bid 3♡ or 3♠.
>
> *Note three, not two.*

This response is forcing. Bid 4♡ or 4♠ if
holding three or more in the suit, otherwise
bid 3NT.

> With a good 11pts or more and a five-card
> *minor* suit, reply in no trumps at the correct
> level. Only bid 3♣ or 3♢ if you are strong
> enough (16pts plus) to play in 5♣ or 5♢.
>
> With less than 11pts, pass an opening 1NT.
> BUT, if you have a weak hand and a five-card
> suit or more, you may bid *two* of it. This is
> known as the weak takeout. It says, 'To play in
> 1NT is pretty hopeless. We shall do better in
> my suit.'
>
> You have to judge this bid. With scattered
> honours about the hand, despite a five-card
> suit, it will usually be better to pass. With a
> six-card suit, and nothing else at all, a two-bid
> must be better than 1NT; you should, with
> luck, make several trump tricks. In between
> these two examples comes the need for
> judgement.
>
> Weak takeouts are 2♢, 2♡ or 2♠, not 2♣,
> which has another meaning (see page 176 for
> 'Stayman', which you should take in at this
> point).

Opener *must* pass a weak takeout.

Now that you have been introduced to the 1NT opening, some of the opening bids you have been making so far will disappear. For obviously there will be hands when you have a choice of opening 1NT or one of a suit.

††† Choose the no-trump opening at all times when holding 12–14pts and no five-card suit. Don't worry about not holding a guard in all four suits – with so few points it is unlikely that you will. If holding five diamonds or five clubs you *may* open 1♢ or 1♣, but 1NT is often superior.

You should *not* open 1NT when:

- you have a singleton;
- you have five hearts or five spades in your hand, when 1♡ or 1♠ is recommended;
- you hold an unbalanced distribution, e.g., 5- 4-2-2.

Other systems force you to pass on 12pts. Playing the weak NT you can strike the first blow with a hand such as QJx Q10xx AQ10x Jx. At best you are getting your side going; at worst you are being a confounded nuisance to the other side.

But be just a little careful. Don't always open 1NT on 12pt hands. A tatty-looking holding like, say, this: K432 K32 K32 K32, is better passed. And don't always reply with 11pts . The 'good' 11pts which you require will contain a share of high intermediate cards, 10s, 9s and 8s, or a five-card minor suit.

As we extol the weak NT we part company with half the bridge players in the land. This other half is the old guard who still play the old-fashioned strong NT opening, usually on 16–18pts. They are missing one of the best bids in bridge.

But you needn't feel sorry for them; feel sorry for yourself instead. The old guard plays a strong no trump, is going to go on playing a strong no trump, and, if you cut one of them as a partner, you'll jolly well have to play a strong no trump too. Seniority has its privileges. The strong no trump is the senior (as are usually its adherents) and you have to give in to it, and them.

So here it is. It doesn't present any difficulties. Just add 3pts to your opening and deduct three from your responses:

*Opener*

*Responder*

Open 1NT on 15–17pts (much better than 16–18).

Bid 2NT on 8pts;
3NT on 9pts plus.

After 2NT from responder bid 3NT with a maximum.

Bid 3♡ or 3♠ with a five-card major suit and 8pts plus.

Reply as in the weak NT.

The weak takeout remains the same.

*Opener's rebid of 1NT* (refer to Chapter 3)

Playing the weak NT your rebid of 1NT:

    1♡ – 1♠
    1NT

is strong, showing exactly 15 or 16pts. You never need to make a weak rebid of 1NT on 13/14pts because the presumption is that you would have opened 1NT in the first place.

But, playing a strong no trump, the rebid of 1NT is weak, 13 or 14pts.

On top of this, strong no trumpers encounter hands which cannot be opened sensibly at all. *You* have no problem with a hand like this:

    ♠Qxxx
    ♡KJx
    ♢Kxx
    ♣Axx

You simply open 1NT. But the strong brigade are in a predicament. They cannot open 1♠ because, if the reply is 2♣, 2♢ or 2♡, they are stuck. A rebid of 2NT would be much too high, as would three of anything, and the four-card spade suit cannot be bid twice.

So they have to fall back on a 'prepared club', with an opening of 1♣ – and hope the rest turns out all right!*

*The prepared club is a bid as described. You will meet players who ask you whether you play the phoney club. You don't. Nor do you wish to learn. But if you are forced into playing a strong no trump, you must be ready to open 1♣ on hands like the above. No other opening is possible.

*Opponents' action after a weak no-trump opening*

If you have a five-card suit and a reasonable number of points, bid the suit. Remember, the opening was a weak one.

With no five-card suit you are frequently in a quandary (which is the intention of the 1NT opener). You may be itching to bid, feeling that your side holds the majority of the points, but cannot think what to say. One course is open to you.

*The double of an opening weak no trump*

†† Unlike the double of a suit, this is for penalties, not for takeout. The opponents need some weapon to punish the effrontery of a player who opens 1NT on 12pts when the cards are stacked in the opposite direction. This is the weapon.

You double with 16pts or more. Partner should pass unless holding a very weak hand of four points or less and a five-card suit, when a takeout into two of the suit should be made.

With this paragraph we diverge from conventional teaching. Traditionally, a weak no trump has been doubled with 14pts (which many players shade down to 13 or even 12). Quite simply, this is not enough strength. Often 1NT doubled is made, and equally often your partner takes out into two of a suit – which is itself doubled for penalties, and goes down.

It may seem weak to pass holding 14 or 15pts, and indeed sometimes you may miss a contract. More often it will work out for the best. Look at it this way: sometimes you may fail to land the fish, but at least you avoid falling into the river.

The double of an opening *strong 1NT* is also for penalties, but rare. If made, partner should not take the double out because of weakness – only if a game appears a more rewarding result, and then jumps to three on a five- or six-card suit.

Finally, when 1NT – weak or strong – is doubled, partner of the opening bidder with a five-card suit should always rescue into two of the suit. Don't, for heaven's sake, rescue on a four-card suit; often as not you will find yourself trying to stem the opposition tide with a total of six paltry trumps.

Obviously a weak no trump is sometimes doubled and suffers a ferocious penalty. Never mind. You must weigh this odd infrequent set-back against the benefits you reap the rest of the time from an opening bid which creates incessant problems for your opponents.

None the less, many players are so alive to the prospect of being doubled that they play a weak no trump non-vulnerable and revert to a strong no trump vulnerable when the penalties are higher (called 'weak and strong' or 'variable'). If they insist, you will have to go along with them too, even if you think their approach rather feeble.

Overleaf is the last of the bidding tables, and it is printed with so many reservations that it was pitch-and-toss whether it appeared in this book. However, it will serve you well if you treat it as a skeleton to be clothed with all the other aspects of bidding, such as:

- your distribution;
- whether you have a 'fit' with your partner;
- your intermediates: 10s, 9s and 8s take tricks, 2s, 3s and 4s don't.

Look at these hands:

♠AKQJxx   ♠1098xxx   Only 22pts, excluding distribution, but
♡xxxxx    ♡A         you must make 7♠ – all 13 tricks. The
◇A        ◇xxxx      distribution and the fit between the two
♣A        ♣xx        hands provide grand slam material.

♠AKQxx    ♠x         26pts this time, but only a slender
♡x        ♡AQJxx     chance of making game in anything,
◇Kxxx     ◇xxxx      unless the defence goes mad.
♣Kxx      ♣Axx

Now take exactly the same hand as the last one, but switch the hearts and diamonds in the East hand so that they look like this:

♠AKQxx    ♠x         Same number of points, but see now
♡x        ♡xxxx      how the fit with your partner in
◇Kxxx     ◇AQJxx     diamonds operates in your favour.
♣Kxx      ♣Axx

You have an easy game, or a respectable slam, in diamonds.

The points tables are needed for precise bids such as limit and no-trump bidding. Otherwise they should be your guide rather than your manacles.

*Opener*

Open one of a suit with 13–20pts.

*Responder*

Raise to the two-level or bid 1NT with 6–10pts.
Raise to the three-level or bid 2NT with 11–12pts.
Raise to the four-level or bid 3NT with 13–15pts.

If changing the suit, make a minimum response

at the one-level with 6–15pts;
at the two-level with 9–15pts and five trumps.

*Opener's rebids*

| | | |
|---|---|---|
| With 13–16pts | i | *To single-raise limit bids* except 1NT – no bid; to 1NT – no bid or a minimum rebid. |
| With 17 or 18pts | | make an encouraging rebid. |
| With 19 or 20pts | | bid game. |
| | ii | *To double-raise limit bids* |
| with 13 or 14pts | | no bid. |
| With 15pts plus | | bid game. |
| | iii | *To change of suit at the one-level* |
| with 13–16pts | | make a minimum rebid. |
| With 17–18pts | | make an encouraging rebid. |
| With 19–20pts | | bid game. |
| | | *At the two-level* |
| with 13–15pts | | make a minimum rebid. |
| With 15–16pts | | make an encouraging rebid. |
| With 17pts plus | | bid game (but see Chapter 7). |

*Responder's rebids*

With 6–10pts no bid (but see Chapter 3).
With 10–12pts bid higher.
With 13–15pts bid the game.

*Opening 1NT*

Bid 1NT on 12–14pts

If partner bids 2NT rebid 3NT if holding 14pts.

Bid 4♡ or 4♠ if holding three of partner's suit, otherwise bid 3NT.

3♣ or 3♢ is forcing as above; support the suit or bid 3NT.

Pass a weak takeout.

Bid 2NT with a good 11 or 12pts.
Bid 3NT with 13pts plus.

Bid 3♡ or 3♠ with 11pts and a five-card (or more) major suit.

Bid 4♡ or 4♠ with 10–16pts and a six-card suit.
With a five-card minor and a good 11pts bid 2NT.
With a five-card minor and a good 12pts plus bid 3NT.
With a five-card minor and 15pts plus bid 3♣ or 3♢.

Make a weak takeout at the two-level on a five-card (or more) suit if judged to be a better contract than 1NT.

## State of play

The remaining provisos are:

● opener must not hold more than 19pts;
● responder must not hold more than 15pts;
● no suit longer than six cards anywhere.

# 7   Big bids on strong hands

It's a big night in the old town tonight and the pies which have satisfied you so far are too tame for such a celebration. The kitchen is getting hotter, but you are not going to stay out of it, not with this dazzling array of kings and aces. It's a magnum of a pie coming up, or even – faint hearts fall out here – a jeroboam.

For now you are about to savour the hands of excellence, and how to manage them. You are setting your sights on the summits of bidding: the slams.

Remind yourself of them:

|  | Non-vul. | Vul. |
|---|---|---|
| A small slam is 6 bid and made, 12 tricks, carrying a bonus of...................... | 500 | 750 |
| A grand slam is 7 bid and made, all the tricks, with a bonus of ........................... | 1000 | 1500 |
| You need about 33pts for a small slam, 37 for a grand slam, but less with good distribution and 'fit'. | | |

The ways to reach these heights are many. For now, only three need concern you:

- the great leap forward, or the jump bid;
- the powerhouse warming up, or the opening bids of two;
- the dash to the top, or Blackwood.

The dash to the top comes first, for a good reason. At the small slam level you can afford to lose only one trick, so how pathetic if the enemy downs you at once by leading out two aces! Blackwood protects you against this calamity.

If either partner bids 4NT after a trump suit has been agreed, one simple question is asked: how many aces have you?

The replies are:

| | | |
|---|---|---|
| 5♣ | none | Easy to remember because the responses |
| 5◇ | one | are upwards from the lowest suit, clubs. |
| 5♡ | two | (5♣ is also the response for four aces.) |
| 5♠ | three | |

The Blackwood 4NT bidder now knows the combined number of aces in the two hands. If two are missing, the brakes will go on and the contract will be halted at the five-level. With aces enough, the small slam is coming up.

Most slams end here, but a Blackwoodsman who scents a grand slam can ask the same question about kings, with a bid of 5NT. The responses are the same: 6♣, no king; 6◇, one; 6♡, two; 6♠, three. This time, if Blackwood reveals a shortage of kings, the bidding will stop at the six-level. With all present and correct the grand-slam summit has been reached.

The Blackwood 4NT is bid after a suit has been agreed:

> directly     1♠ – 3♠
> 4NT (Blackwood)
>
> or by inference  1♠ – 4NT (Blackwood)

But sometimes 4NT is not Blackwood:

> 1NT – 4NT

No suit has been mentioned, let alone agreed. What this bid means will be explained later. Meanwhile nearly all bids of 4NTs are Blackwood, and we shall not confuse you here with further exceptions.

## The great leap forward, or the jump bid

You already know of jump bids in the same suit such as 1♠ – 3♠, which simply express the limit of a responder's hand and are not forcing. Now you are about to make the more heady jump in a *new* suit.

*Responder*

You will have noticed that until now our discussion has been limited to hands containing 15pts or fewer.

When you hold 16 or more points you must say so immediately with a change of suit and a jump to the next level: (Opening 1♡) – 3♣. You may have a powerful club suit, you may not. No matter. It is crucial to show the points at once. The trump suit can sort itself out later. So:

(Opening 1♡):    ♠A x
                 ♡Q 10 x x
                 ◇A K x x
                 ♣K x x   bid 3◇

Of course, you already know that partner can make 4♡, but what about 6♡ or even 7♡? If you make a feeble response of 4♡, your partner may pass and any possible slam has gone beyond recall.

† One thing is certain about the great leap forward. With a combined 29pts neither partner must allow the bidding to stop before game is called. And the minimum of 29pts in the two hands, given a fit, is already nudging a slam. If either player has extra values, the Blackwood dash to the top will get under way.

*Opener*

After a jump response, rebid naturally at the lowest level; your suit (with five), a reasonable second suit, support for your partner, or a rebid in no trumps. But with more than a minimum opening, say 16pts or more, you will at least be thinking of a slam. Be careful in this case not to close down the bidding with 3NT.

*Responder*

When you jumped, you bid your 16pts. Don't ††
bid them twice. On the hand above, if the
bidding goes:

1♡ – 3♣
3♡    settle for 4♡.

But even with an extra queen, you would be
worth a Blackwood 4NT.

Opener

You too can make jump bids to show strength.

Your range for an opening one of a suit is
13–20pts. You may feel a little tense about
opening at the one-level on 19 or 20pts, for fear
that partner will pass. Don't be. If partner has
less than 6pts you are unlikely to miss a game.

Conversely, if partner does reply, you want
to be sure of game. You may be able to bid it
yourself:

1♡ – 1♠
3NT

or you may not:

♠Axx
♡AKJxx
♢x
♣AKJx

On this hand, after 1♡–1♠ you need further
information before calling game, or possibly
going for a slam.

Force with 3♣.

*Responder*

Now, with even a depressing 6pts you must not only bid again, but also keep the bidding open to game. With a minimum 6 or 7pts, make a minimum rebid. Of course, though, if you have a fair hand you will show it. And if you can count 12pts or more on top of your partner's forcing bid you are in the slam zone.

## The powerhouse warming up, or the opening bids of two

Acol opening bids of two are strong – in different ways. They fall into three categories:

2NT, an all-rounder with plenty of points;
2♣, the emperor of all opening bids;
2◇, 2♡ or 2♠, strong hands usually with good distribution, or one solid or near-solid suit.

## Opening 2NT

A balanced hand with 20–22pts.

*Responder*

Bid 3NT with 4pts plus; pass with less.
Bid 3♡ or 3♠ with a five-card suit or more, and 4pts plus.
Bid 4♡ or 4♠ only with a with a six-card suit or longer and no slam interest.

To 3♡ or 3♠, rebid 4♡ or 4♠ with three cards in the suit, otherwise 3NT.

Only bid 3◇ on an unbalanced hand with at least 8pts, or in search of a slam. (Do not reply 3♣; this is a speciality bid you will come to later.) To an opening 2NT there is no weak takeout.

## Opening 2♣

This is the hand that makes you feel all's right with the world. The 2♣ bid is conventional; it does not mean you have any clubs, but in most cases promises 23pts at least.

### Responder

However wretched your hand, keep in mind that your partner is very strong. You must keep the bidding going until game is reached. The action you take facing 2♣ is:

- with less than 1½ quick tricks* make a conventional denial bid of 2◇ (but see Chapter 17);
- with 1½ quick tricks or more, but no five-card suit, respond 2NT;
- with 1½ quick tricks or more and a five-card suit respond 2♡, 2♠, 3♣ or 3◇. Do not jump the bidding; there is no hurry.

After the response (usually 2◇) the opener begins to clarify the hand, generally by bidding a suit at the lowest level, say 2♠.

---

*Quick tricks are high cards which take tricks quickly:

> An ace is 1 quick trick
> A K is 2 .    K Q is 1
> A Q is 1½    K x is ½

That is all of them. The A K Q is not three; the queen is not quick enough.

*Responder*

With no other feasible bid, make another denial with 2NT. But because your partner is so strong you must bid any feature you have, for instance:

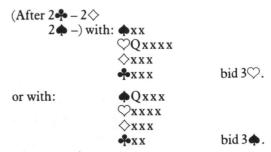

(After 2♣ – 2◇
    2♠ –) with:  ♠xx
           ♡Qxxxx
           ◇xxx
           ♣xxx        bid 3♡.

or with:        ♠Qxxx
           ♡xxxx
           ◇xxx
           ♣xx         bid 3♠.

And use your common sense. If you have less than 1½ quick tricks and a fair hand, bid it:

After: 2♣ – 2◇
    2♠:   ♠xx
        ♡K 10xxx
        ◇K J xxx
        ♣x
                    bid 3♡;

then after 3NT        bid 4◇.

Keep the pot boiling.

The only time an opening 2♣ can be allowed to die short of game is when the opener has a balanced hand and exactly 23 or 24pts, then:

    2♣ – 2◇
    2NT

responder can pass with under 2pts.

It follows that opener with 25 or 26pts and no reasonable suit must bid

    2♣ – 2◇
    3NT.

## The powerhouse warming up, part 2: the strong twos

Opening two-bids, other than 2♣, are strong but in a different way. They guarantee to take eight tricks without any help from partner; and almost always contain a six-card trump suit:

*a* ♠AKQJxx    *b* ♠AQJxxx
  ♡x    *or*    ♡KQJ10x
  ♢AKx      ♢x
  ♣xxx      ♣x

Played in spades, the first hand has eight *playing* tricks, six trumps and two diamonds. The second has nine playing tricks, five trumps and four hearts.

In each case open 2♠.

### Responder

The strong twos must be kept open for one round (but see note*).

With less than 1½ quick tricks bid a negative 2NT (but see Chapter 17).

With less than 1½ tricks, but holding 10/11pts and a guard in all the other three suits, bid 3NT.

---

*All bridge players keep a 2♣ bid open but some prefer to pass the strong twos when holding very little. We won't bother with reasons for this latter behaviour, but we will state that we don't agree with it. For instance, the two-suit hand above (*b*) screams for an opportunity to rebid the heart suit. Enough to say that you can insist on getting the negative 2NT reply by saying to your partner before play begins, 'Keep my twos open'.

With 1½ quick tricks or more bid anything else, but give absolute priority to supporting your partner's suit:

(Opening 2♠):   ♠xxx
              ♡Kx
              ◇AQJxx
              ♣xxx          bid 3♠.

Even if you have to bid a negative 2NT you may be able to support your partner on the next round:

2♠ – 2NT   ♠Kxx
              ♡Jxxxx
              ◇xxxx
              ♣x

3♠ – 4♠

But if you have nothing to say after your negative 2NT you may pass on the next round.

## Department of warnings

It seems like a long time since you picked up an opening bid. Your cards have been abysmal. You have played and lost a couple of rubbers. Suddenly you are dealt a 25pt hand.

## Warning no. 1

You have a thrilling, a beautiful hand; perhaps, you are thinking, a slam hand.

Keep cool. Your partner opposite may hold only one point. If so, you have 26 between you, the same as if you picked up 13pts each. It is not yet time to get excited.

## Warning no. 2

You open the bidding with 1♠ and your partner replies 3◇. This is the big one! Surely a slam is coming. Isn't it Blackwood time?

Look again. You opened with 14pts. Despite your partner's raise you still have only 14pts. Take it easy with a minimum bid.

Bid your own hand, not your partner's.

**Warning no. 3**

Your partner opens 2NT and you hold 13pts including a string of top spades. This *is* a slam hand. Do you communicate the joyful news with a bid of 4♠?

You don't. There is no hurry. You need time and space to explore for the final contract, 6♠ or 7♠. Bid 3♠; any bid facing 2NT is forcing.

In the course of strong bidding it is nearly always unnecessary to jump. Nothing is more irritating than a sequence like

$$1\heartsuit - 2♠$$
$$4♠$$

when opener could perfectly well have bid 3♣.

Bids to game are weaker than simple raises. 2NT–4♠ means 'I                    †
have no aces, and a hand just about able to take ten tricks. Stop here. No slam.' 2NT–3♠ may be minimum, or enormous. There is a chance next time round to say which.

Jump bids short of game as:

$$2♣ - 2\diamondsuit$$
$$3\heartsuit$$

carry conventional meanings which you need not worry about yet.

So, however strong you are, go along peacefully at first. Don't rush. And if you do meet a partner who passes 2NT–3♠, try to raise a smile – and then go and find another partner.

The last strong bids in this chapter are openings of 4♡ or 4♠. In these cases you sometimes have an option of opening 2♡ or 2♠, but you have a reason for leaping straight to four. The commoner of the two is 4♡:

♠x
♡A K Q x x x x
♢K J x
♣x x

With at least one of the opposition to bid you are afraid they will find a game in 4♠. Your blanket bid of 4♡ is an attempt to head them off.

Equally an opening bid of 4♠ is an attempt to stifle a game bid in another suit.

*Responder*

Pass unless holding four quick tricks; then a
Blackwood 4NT would be a sensible reply.

During an evening's bridge there will usually be quite a few small
slams about. Most are not difficult to bid. *Your* difficulty may be that,
because the really good hands come infrequently, and the superlative
ones less often still, you may forget the ground rules. Or you may, at
first, think that bids of six or seven are only for the superstars. They
aren't.

Psychologically, it may seem a daunting step to go on from a
comfortable game to a slam. But like P. G. Wodehouse's golfer, who
claimed to have been put off his stroke by the roaring of butterflies in a
nearby meadow, it is only in the mind. When you are offered a
magnum of champagne, don't brush it aside and settle for a bottle.
Take it, and the bonuses too.

**State of play**

Almost there. Only exclude hands with seven-card or more suits.

# 8  Refining the play

Checking up on the ingredients for a fruit pie, or a megapie as in the last section, is much easier than making it; especially with rival cooks in the kitchen throwing in pepper and salt and in many ways trying to divert you from your purpose.

So now we are back with playing the cards. In bridge much more time is spent in cardplay than in bidding. Bidding is no more than an overture to the main work in which the duel between the declarer and the two defenders is fought. It is here that skill and ingenuity win the day, and ineptitude meets defeat.

You and the expert will often land in the same contract of three no trumps or four spades. There the comparison ends, for most beginners are so fascinated by the bidding that they pay only peremptory attention to the play of the cards. Yet it is the cardplay which is the real fascination.

The play's the thing, and we recommend at this point that you reread Chapters 2 and 4 which contain the fundamentals of cardplay. Without them you will be under a constant handicap and in danger of missing the real fun of the game.

Probably, impatient to go forward, you won't take this advice. So, with no apologies, we extract one or two important matters with which to refresh your memory.

Declarer: pause when dummy goes down, see your two hands as a whole, count your potential tricks, and make a plan. Aim to make your contract either with finesses, by ruffing in dummy or by setting up a side suit.

Defenders: know your opening leads by heart. Signal, and watch your partner's signals. Don't give unnecessary tricks away.

Bridge is not a game in which you can rely upon being given second chances, like serving at tennis. One error by the declarer can lose a contract; one error by the defence can give it away.

Now for one or two new facets of the play.

**Holding up**

When an opponent leads a king there is no law that says you must immediately put an ace on it. You want to take tricks when it suits you, not at the command of the other side.

*Declarer's hold-ups*

In Chapter 4 we showed how declarer playing in no trumps usually holds up an ace to prevent the defence from running off a suit. For the same reason you should generally hold up

†   with A K x:

```
            x x
        ┌───────┐
Q (led) │       │ x (played)
        └───────┘
            A K x
```

If there is no danger elsewhere, first play low. Even though you stop the suit twice, it may still be brought in to defeat your contract.

You do *not* hold up if by doing so you sacrifice a trick:

```
            J x
        ┌───────┐
K (led) │       │ x
        └───────┘
            A 10 x
```

Put up the ace; you are assured of a second trick in the suit.

Nor do you hold up if a suit other than the one led presents a greater danger:

♠xxx
♡xxx
◇AKJxx
♣xx

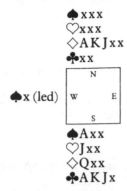

♠x (led)

♠Axx
♡Jxx
◇Qxx
♣AKJx

Play the spade ace at once, take your five diamond tricks and risk the club finesse for nine tricks. Nothing could be more mortifying than to play low and watch helplessly while the opponents switch to hearts and take four or five tricks in that suit.

One specific hold-up involves all three players at the table. That is when the king is led from K Q 10 and some others against no trumps:

x

K (led)       x

AJx

The declarer holds up and takes two tricks if the suit is continued. It won't be. The player who led should see the danger and switch to another suit.

It follows that if the cards lie:

$$x x$$

K (led) ☐ J x x

A x x

partner holding the jack must throw it under the king to indicate that it is safe to continue the suit.

The same sequence arises when the queen is led from Q J 9; on the lead of the queen partner is expected to contribute the 10.

### Defence hold-ups

Both these examples are in no-trump contracts.

**1** To prevent declarer from making a suit:

♠x x
♡x x x
♢K Q J 10 x (dummy)
♣x x x

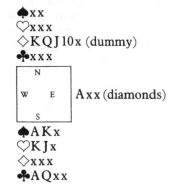

A x x (diamonds)

♠A K x
♡K J x
♢x x x
♣A Q x x

3NT cannot be made without the diamond suit. East must hold up the ace to cut declarer off from dummy.

2 To keep control of a suit:     ††

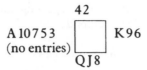

42

A 10 7 5 3     K 96
(no entries)
        Q J 8

As West you lead the 5. Partner takes the king and returns the 9, covered by declarer's jack. If you put up the ace now and return a small one you will blow the defence. You have no entries and your partner has none of your suit left. Let the jack win. Your partner, if on lead, will then be able to lead your suit again.

**Ducking**

Holding up is a negative procedure to prevent the other side from making tricks. Ducking is positive, to take tricks for yourself. In this hand 3NT is the contract:

♠xxx
♡xx
◇AKxxx
♣Jxx

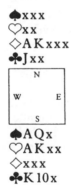

♠AQx
♡AKxx
◇xxx
♣K 10 x

The diamond suit cannot be established by playing out AKx because dummy has no entries.

Duck. Instead of losing the third trick, declarer loses the *first* by playing low from each hand, so retaining a card to play to dummy later.

## Unblocking

At its simplest, unblocking means getting out of partner's way. It can apply to either declarer or defenders.

*Defence unblocks*

Your partner leads a king (from K Q or K Q J). You hold A x. Generally you should overtake with your ace and play your small one back. Playing against a suit contract you are preparing to take the third trick in the suit, either with partner's jack or with a ruff in your hand. And against no trumps? Your partner will have led from K Q J x and perhaps more. If you don't overtake you will block the suit on the second round with the ace.

The same applies if you hold K x and the queen is led by your partner.

However, with more than two in the suit, say K 8 2 or A 8 2, don't overtake. Signal the honour by playing the 8.

Blocking and unblocking, holding up and ducking are complex subjects about which whole books have been written. This is an outline only, but really all such manoeuvres come down to one word: think. If you think and go wrong, maybe next time you will get it right. If you don't think at all you are not playing bridge.

There is almost no play of the cards to which the words 'always' or 'never' can be attached. Bridge is a game of infinite variety and millions of combinations of cards. By now you should have sufficient understanding of the cards to treat some of our earlier advice with flexibility.

Second player plays low. Yes, but:

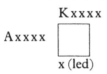

K x x x x

A x x x x

x (led)

The chances are that declarer is leading a singleton. Go up with your ace or you may never make it.

KQx

Axx ▢

x (led)

No hurry to play the ace now. Play low.

KJx

Axx ▢

x (led)

Criminal to play the ace. Declarer may intend to finesse the jack to your partner's queen.

Third player plays high. Yes, but:

QJ109x

x (led) ▢ Kxxx

If you play the king it will be taken by declarer's ace and the whole suit established in dummy. Play low; if declarer has Ax or Axx you will still retain control with the king after three rounds.

Third player plays high in all ordinary circumstances:

xxx

x (led) ▢ KJx

Play the king; don't finesse against your partner. Yes, but:

Qxx

x (led) ▢ K10x

Your partner has not led away from the ace (a partner who has should return with ignominy to Chapter 2). If you put up the king it will certainly lose to declarer's ace, and the queen will be a trick in dummy.

But your partner may have led from the jack. Play the 10. It cannot cost anything, and may succeed.

You have also reached a stage when you may lead away from an ace at a judicious moment during the play of the hand, but not at any old moment:

K J x

A x x
(on lead)

Your partner may hold the queen. If you lead low the declarer is on a guess whether to put up the king or the jack.

But treat with care. If dummy shows nothing:

x x x

A x x

hold on to your ace and keep holding on until your partner or declarer leads the suit, or until you can bang it out to defeat the contract.

You have not been given a licence to rush out with unsupported aces at every opportunity.

## The fourth highest and the rule of eleven

The lead of the fourth highest of a suit carries an inbuilt message of great significance. The message may appear complex, but it is unravelled by simple arithmetic.

Whichever card is led, deduct the pips on it from 11 and the difference is the number of higher cards in that suit held by the other three hands.

An example will make it clearer:

A J 7 (dummy)

5 (led)        Q 8 2

Sitting with the Q 8 2 you take 5 from 11. Of the six cards higher than your partner's 5 you can see five of them, three in dummy and two in your hand. That leaves only one for the declarer who, being the declarer, is most likely to hold the king.

Now see how useful that information is. If the 7 is played from dummy you need only insert your 8 to draw out declarer's king, retaining the Q 2 over dummy's A J. You have gained a trick.

Of course the declarer too applies the rule of eleven, but in this case not so usefully. After you have played your 8 declarer is aware that you have one card higher than the 5, but only you know that it is the queen.

And note this: if, surprisingly, your partner holds the king and your 8 is taken by the 9 or 10, nothing is lost. Put the cards down and work it out for yourself.

Now we will show the full suit, and suppose you were the player who made the opening lead of the 5:

AJ7

109653      Q82

K4

When next you play the suit you must play the 3. The logic is simple. If the 5 was the fourth highest, the 3 must be your fifth, showing your partner a five-card suit. If you play a card higher than the one you led you can only hold a four-card suit.

For your own sake, return to this page until you are sure of its contents. A knowledge of the rule of eleven will mean that no longer will your partner's lead of a fourth highest be a lowly card of no significance. It may carry enough information to sway the battle.

**Now a short note on dummy**

Short, because dummy's rights are limited to ensuring that declarer 1 plays from the correct hand and 2 follows suit. As dummy, you can say to a declarer whose card is beginning to come from the wrong hand, 'Other hand, partner,' or to one who fails to follow suit (in bridge, revoking), 'Having no more, partner.' Otherwise dummy remains silent and (in rubber bridge) does not touch the cards.

**State of play**

No change.

# 9 Double time

Remember our assertion that the most rewarding doubles in bridge are those at a low level:

$2\diamondsuit$

$1\heartsuit$ ⬚ double

††† With reasonable diamonds and some outside points, do not hesitate to double for penalties.

The three daggers appear because beginners find this hard to believe. They think that the higher the other side bids, the more likely it is to go down. Quite false. No couple in their senses will bid a grand slam unless it is there or about there, certainly not if it is four or five tricks short. But plenty of players (not you by this time!) go crazy in the head about 13pts and chip in with $2\diamondsuit$ as above. Such idiotic bids deserve the full doubling treatment.

In general, you make penalty doubles when your partner has bid – not often all on your own.

You may at first be puzzled when you hold hands like this:

$1\heartsuit$

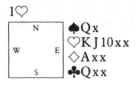

♠Q x
♡K J 10 x x
♢A x x
♣Q x x

Don't be. Aside from the fact that a double now is for takeout – you can't have it both ways! – who says that you can beat $1\heartsuit$ by taking seven tricks? Pass, and await developments.

And do not be misled by hands in which you appear to have four certain tricks against $4\heartsuit$ or $4\spadesuit$, say A K and two aces. Declarer may easily have a singleton and deny you your fourth trick. Don't double.

† Particularly, do not be misled into doubling on hands with five

straggly trumps in the declarer's suit and an outside trick. Put yourself in the opponents' position. They have bid a perfectly respectable:

$$1\heartsuit - 3\heartsuit$$
$$4\heartsuit$$

and out of nowhere you come in with a penalty double. You might as well send the declarer a note saying, 'I have all the trumps,' for there is nothing else you could be doubling on. Knowing this, declarer – in the light of the information you have given – will play the hand differently and smoothly pick up your trumps and make the contract.

In fact you should rarely double for one down. The arithmetic is against you. If you succeed, you gain an extra 50 or 100; if the contract is made in say $4\heartsuit$, the declarer gains an extra 170 – scoring 290 instead of 120 – and it is more likely to be made after you have given away the position of the key cards.

Do *not* double if the opponents can get out into another contract which they can make. Do *not* double slams, unless they have been reached by competitive bidding. You can double a grand slam with the ace of trumps!

Sensibly, you must take account of the opposition bidding and your partner's possible holding, before doubling. Then, when you are sure, jump hard on opponents who overbid.

However, that may not be the end of it. Suppose, when both sides are bidding, your partner doubles, sending the message, 'They can't make it.' Most of the time you must believe it, and pass. But occasionally you will have a hand – usually a long trump suit and little else – which offers no defensive tricks; then you can exercise your judgement to take the double out by rebidding your suit. This is tricky ground which you will learn to tread with experience.

### Redoubling
This is yah-boo stuff. An opponent doubles, saying, 'You can't make it.' You redouble, replying, 'Yes, I can.' Any score now, a penalty or a contract made, is quadrupled. Up in the stratosphere, you had better be *quite* sure of what you are doing!

A redouble also has a conventional meaning, as described in Chapter 5.

### State of play
No change.

# 10　Big bids on weak hands

Now the kitchen is getting hotter still.

It is your turn to say something, and frankly what you are looking at doesn't impress you – a large number of plums, not even of the top quality, and little else. You have a strong suspicion that the enemy, when it gets together, can concoct a pie in apples, damsons or even mixed fruits. *Nil desperandum.* What you are going to do is to try to sabotage this by laying down a barrage.

The barrage is a big opening bid on a weak hand containing a seven-card suit at least. The number of points is of little importance:

♠x
♡xxx
◇KJ10xxxx
♣Kx

Opening bid: 3◇.

It is known as a weak three, a pre-emptive bid because it pre-empts the opponents from bidding peacefully between themselves; or more hopefully a shutout bid because it may shut the other side out of the bidding altogether.

The yardstick for the opening is that you should not go more than 500 down if you are doubled and your partner has nothing; that is, three down non-vulnerable or two down vulnerable. So, non-vulnerable:

♠x
♡xx
◇xxx
♣KQJ10xxx

will do for an opening 3♣. Vulnerable, you ought (by the book) to have a little more.

In practice weak threes are often opened with less, but never much stronger. For instance:

♠AQxxxxx
♡x
◇KJxx
♣x

is much too good. On this hand you open 1♠; if your partner has an ace and something in spades you should make four. Weak openings are weak bids on weak hands. They have no pretensions other than to irritate and disorganize the opposition.

So do not open a weak three if you have a prospect of game.   ††

Partner of the weak-three opener passes with less than 16pts. Make no   †††
mistake about this. Even with 13 or 14pts, and however pretty the hand, say no bid.

With 16pts or more bid *game* in your partner's suit. Don't worry   ††
even if you have only a singleton trump; your partner has plenty. For other bids by responder, see Chapter 19.

Do not bid 3NT with 16pts unless you have at least three cards in   ††
your partner's suit, and then only if the opening was a minor, 3♣ or 3◇. With three hearts or spades you must bid 4♡ or 4♠.

Without three cards in partner's suit, playing in no trumps, you may never get into dummy to make the long suit.

To make these points clear:

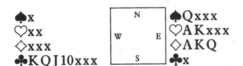

♠x                        ♠Qxxx
♡xx          N            ♡AKxxx
◇xxx       W   E          ◇AKQ
♣KQJ10xxx     S           ♣x

West opens 3♣, and East should bid 5♣ which is made easily, losing a club and a spade. But an East who bids 3NT is in a hopeless position. Not a single trick will be made in clubs. And do get this right: only the club suit is of interest to the partnership. An East who bids 3♡ should be recommended to a good psychiatrist; such a bid promises a self-contained heart suit, the values for a game and possibly a slam, and is unconditionally forcing.

It is no secret that a weak-three opening is a weak bid. Everyone who plays bridge knows it, and that includes the opponents. They are aware that they are being upstaged, but doing something about it is another matter. What they would have liked was a cosy sequence like this:

$$1\heartsuit - 1\spadesuit$$
$$2\heartsuit - 3\heartsuit$$
$$4\heartsuit$$

but they have been foiled by your rude opening of 3♣ and now have to start bidding up in the far yonder, at least at the three-level. Very frustrating, particularly should there be a possible slam in the hand. They have been robbed of two rounds of exploratory bidding.

So be it. An opponent with a sound hand and a good suit can only bid it over a pre-empt, 3♠, or 4♠ if strong enough. But what about a good hand without a biddable suit?

In this case partner must be asked to bid, and there are several ways of doing it. We recommend a double for takeout, the same as over a one-bid. To make it you need the values for an opening bid, perhaps less with a distribution of 5-5-4 or 4-4-4-1. Partner, of course, must reply with a suit, and if holding a reasonable hand must jump the bidding to game to show better than a forced reply.

†† 

That is all there should be to it, but it isn't. Even experts disagree on the best bid to make for takeout over a weak three. Some dislike the double, preferring to keep it for penalties. Others will play nothing else. There are four popular takeout systems, listed below, and this will surely convince you that, when numerous alternatives are put forward to counteract a bid, the bid itself must be a good one. True. The opening weak three is a good bid.

One other point about takeout doubles. You will hear them referred to as optional doubles, meaning that responder *can* exercise the option to pass if holding nothing but strength in the opener's suit:

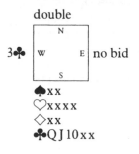

```
            double
          ┌────────┐
          │   N    │
  3♣      │ W    E │   no bid
          │   S    │
          └────────┘
          ♠xx
          ♡xxxx
          ◇xx
          ♣QJ10xx
```

South can pass, so translating a takeout into a penalty double. But it rarely happens, and to pass you must hold *strength* in the opening suit. With:

♠xxxx
♡x
◇xxxx
♣Jxxx

you must bid 3♠.

Takeout systems over a weak-three opening:

- double (can be passed, but it is really a takeout double);
- 3NT, sometimes 3◇ over 3♣ and 3NT over anything else;
- Fishbein (or Herbert), bid one suit higher than the pre-empt, i.e. 3◇ over 3♣;
- lower minor, 3◇ over 3♣; 4♣ over anything else.

These are for the record. Luckily for you the double is nowadays the most commonly played.

Before beginning to play with an unknown partner you have several matters to agree. These are the questions you need to ask:

1 What no trump do you play? (You play weak.)

2 What is your takeout bid over threes? (Yours is a double.)

3 What do you lead from A K? Many players lead the king. We see no merit in it because the king is led from both A K and from K Q and becomes an ambiguous card. But there it is. You are not in the business of correcting players, only understanding, which is why you ask the question. You yourself can continue to lead the ace.

The questions, always asked by one partner or the other, can be put into shorthand: 'Weak, double, ace, all right?' Partner will agree or not. And you also add, 'Keep my twos open.' That is a command, not a question.

### State of play

From now on deal and play naturally without alteration to the hands.

# 11   Spotlight on declarer

The plums are assembled, the pastry made and the pie put in the oven. The chef relaxes. The weary work is done and nothing can now go wrong . . . until suddenly the gas goes out.

Plum pie has become the target of industrial action.

The chef is aggrieved, but it is no great hassle. There are contingency plans for such events. The pie can be taken next door to a friendly neighbour and cooked by electricity; it can be shelved, and·a can of peaches opened in its place; the dinner party can be cancelled, or the guests taken out instead to the local Café des Trois Atouts.

Murphy's Law is this: if anything can go wrong, it will go wrong. It is a sensible starting point for a declarer. Count the winners, count the losers, make a plan, and then ask the silent question, 'But what if . . .?'

For instance, your trumps are like this:

K9xx

AQ10xx

A beautiful suit, but what if . . . one defender has Jxxx and the other none?

Keep your options open by leading first a high card from the hand with two honours, in this case the ace. If either defender has a void you can finesse against the jack in either direction, and lose no trick in the suit. Had you played the king first you would have surrendered one of your options, the finesse through the K9.

Another example:

♠KJxx
♡QJ10x
◇Kx
♣xxx

♠A10xxx
♡AKx
◇Ax
♣Kxx

You are in 4♠ and a diamond is led. Even if a spade is lost the hand looks set fair with four spade winners, four hearts and two diamonds. With nine trumps your natural play is to lead the AK, hoping to drop the queen.

But what if . . . East has three spades to the queen, takes the third round and nastily switches to the club queen? You may lose a spade and three clubs.

Really, there is no problem. East is the danger hand, so East must not be allowed to lead. First lead the *spade* king and then finesse the 10 towards West. For all you care West can win with the queen. A club lead from there will not harm you; nor will any other lead. Later you can discard a losing club on the fourth heart, and make certain of your contract.

Always look to see which hand may be the danger, and play, if you ††† can, to keep it out of the lead.

Now we want to revert to some of the earlier advice in Chapter 4 on playing the hand, reaffirming some points, and clothing the skeletons of others.

Our first reminder – yes, again! – is about the declarer's pause when dummy is spread on the table. An expert, even with a magnitude of knowledge and experience, never sets about a hand without making an assessment of it, so why should lesser mortals dash straight into the play?

Half a second simply will not do to count your tricks, plan the play and (since the last page) ask yourself the question, 'What if . . .?'

You cannot, of course, squat at the table like a stuffed frog in a reverie, but you will be surprised how long a pause of twenty seconds seems in a bridge room. Discipline yourself to take a reasonable time, even if the other players begin to fidget. It is your entitlement.

We are fully aware that most of you will not heed this advice. The cards are down, the hunt is up, the adrenalin is flowing, and it seems no occasion for dalliance. Nonetheless, dally you must if you want to play this game well.

Our second reminder – count your tricks – will probably seem as tedious as the first. But:

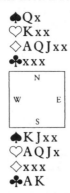

♠Qx
♡Kxx
♢AQJxx
♣xxx

♠KJxx
♡AQJx
♢xxx
♣AK

You are in 3NT and a club is led. You take the trick, reach for a diamond and prepare to finesse. After all, you always try to establish your long suit when playing in no trumps.

But 'always' is a dangerous word in bridge. This is an easy hand, but a tricky one with which many players will go wrong. You could ask 'What if . . . East holds K10xx in diamonds?' and the answer would be that only eight tricks can be made before the opponents get in and run off the clubs. One down.

By all means ask 'What if . . .?' but even before that the discipline is to *count your tricks*. All you had to do with this hand was to play a spade at trick 2 and help yourself to two spades, four hearts, a diamond and two clubs. It was unbeatable, provided you left the diamonds alone.

In the last hand the diamonds were held against you twice. In this one they aren't:

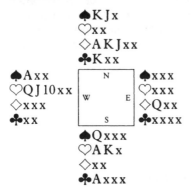

♠KJx
♡xx
♢AKJxx
♣Kxx

♠Axx
♡QJ10xx
♢xxx
♣xx

♠xxx
♡xxx
♢Qxx
♣xxxx

♠Qxxx
♡AKx
♢xx
♣Axxx

You are in 3NT and the *heart* queen is led.

You hold up once and the heart is continued. Count your tricks, for a very important principle is involved. After the diamond finesse is lost (which you must assume) and the hearts are cleared, you have eight tricks before losing a spade. At that point West will win and you will be one down, losing a diamond, a spade and three hearts.

In such cases, and they are frequent, you must first attack the possible entry in the danger hand; or to put it another way you must look to take your ninth trick immediately, while it is still safe to do so.

So play a spade *first*. It doesn't matter whether the ace goes up or not, for now you have the ninth trick in the bag and can switch to diamonds. Your hold-up in hearts has ensured that after you have lost the diamond finesse East will have no heart to return.

This is really a reminder on its own. Always think of the danger hand, and how you can prevent it from winning the lead at the wrong moment.

♠10xxx
♡xxx
◇AQx
♣KQx

♠KQJxx
♡xxx
◇Kx
♣Axx

You are in 4♠ and a club is led. You have ten tricks, four spades, three diamonds and three clubs. Are you going to follow the rule about drawing trumps first?

Look again. Count your losers, a spade and three hearts. You must quickly play A K Q of diamonds and throw a losing heart before tackling the trumps.

It is an old saying that the Embankment is populated by players who failed to draw trumps. If this is so, quite a sizeable part of it is reserved for those who did so, without thinking.

Reminder no. 3 *is* to draw trumps first, unless there is a reason not to; a play such as the last one or a plan to ruff in dummy. But even if you do intend to take ruffs in dummy, draw some trumps first if you can afford to:

♠Qxxx
♡x
♢Qxx
♣xxxxx

You are in 6♠, a laydown contract after you have ruffed two hearts in dummy. The only possible danger is an overruff of the third heart. You have plenty of trumps. Play out ♠A K first before ruffing.

♠AKxxxx
♡Axx
♢AKx
♣x

Now here is the other side of the coin, the *crossruff*, one of the most satisfying plays in bridge. It sends a glow through you and confounds the opposition.

Far from drawing trumps first, you will often not draw any at all. Your aim is to make most or all of your trumps separately in your hand and in dummy. The play is new to you, so follow this hand carefully:

♠Axxxx
♡x
♢Q1098
♣Kxx

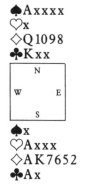

You have bid to 6♢ and a spade is led. Playing the hand straightforwardly, the contract is out of sight.

♠x
♡Axxx
♢AK7652
♣Ax

If you ruff hearts in dummy, and spades in your own hand, however, a feast of tricks will be cooking.

But first two rules apply to crossruff hands.

† 1 You must take the tricks in your fourth suit, in this case the A K of clubs, at the beginning; otherwise as you crossruff the defenders may throw clubs and score a wounding ruff against you.

2 You must, at the right stage, ruff high. If at any time you are †
overruffed, a trump will be returned and your contract sunk
without trace.

So in this hand, take the spade lead and ruff a spade. Then the play
goes: *club* king, *club* ace, *heart* ace, heart ruff, spade ruff, heart ruff,
spade ruff with the king, heart ruff with the queen, spade ruff with the
ace.

That is eleven tricks, and the last one will be made between
declarer's *diamond* 7 and dummy's *diamond* 10.

Provided you remember to ruff high, this is lovely stuff. The
opposition is remorselessly ground to pieces, powerless to interfere
with the rhythm of your play.

Powerless in all ways but one. Once you get going you are unstop-
pable but, just as a false note can ruin a chord, so an opening trump
lead may tear your symphony to pieces. That is one for you to
remember when you are playing in defence and sense a crossruff
coming.

Reminder no. 4 is on setting up a side suit for discards. The example
we gave in Chapter 4 was of a suit ready-made for discards; but you
may have to do some work to get your suit going:

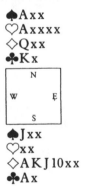

♠Axx
♡Axxxx
◇Qxx
♣Kx

You are in 5◇, facing two losers in
spades and one in hearts. Don't
waste time bemoaning 3NT; be
grateful that the opening lead was a
club and not a spade. Your side
suit is hearts.

♠Jxx
♡xx
◇AKJ10xx
♣Ax

Take the club lead in your hand with the ace. Draw two rounds of
trumps with the AK, then play ace and another heart which loses.
Win the likely spade return in dummy, ruff another heart with the 10.
If the hearts were 3-3 you now have two left in dummy for spade
discards, and you will make 6◇. If they were 4-2, cross to dummy
with the trump queen and ruff another heart with the jack. Your club
king is the entry for the last heart on which you can discard one spade;
you make 5◇.

The crucial factor in this line of play is to ensure enough entries in dummy, which is why you took the opening lead in your own hand. Which means that you planned it all before play began, during the pause . . . but you have heard about that before!

Reminder no. 5 is on finessing.

**1** With cards like these:

> J x facing A Q 10 x
>
> *or*
>
> 9 x x facing A Q J 10 x

beginners tend to forget the merit of leading the high card from hand, in these cases the 9 or jack, and running it. If it is not covered and the finesse succeeds, you can repeat it.

If you lead low and finesse the 10 you will win just the same if the king is on your left, but now you are stuck in the wrong hand.

†† Of course, you can return to the other hand with an entry and finesse again. But the more experienced you become at bridge the more you will realize that entries are precious. Far from growing on trees, they either grow sparsely and need nourishing, or sometimes they don't exist at all.

**2** In almost all everyday situations, when you are going to finesse, as in this example:

> A 10 x          K J x x x

first play the ace or king, and then finesse. This gives you one extra chance, that the queen is singleton and may drop.

**3** With these cards:

> x x x          A Q 10

and no knowledge of where the king may be, usually take the deep finesse of the 10. If you need *three* tricks in the suit you must finesse the 10.

**4** And now for a new finesse, the most pleasing of them all:

♠AQJx      Your are in 5◇ and in danger of
♡KJx      losing three club tricks. But no
◇Jxx      danger exists because you are
♣xxx      about to take a *ruffing finesse*.

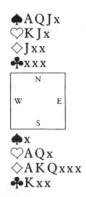

♠x
♡AQx
◇AKQxxx
♣Kxx

Draw trumps and play a spade, but not to finesse in the ordinary way.
Put up the ace and lead the queen back. If East puts up the king, ruff,
return to dummy and throw a club on the spade jack. If the king does
not appear, throw a club and let West win. You still have the *spade*
jack to take care of a losing club.

As you can see, a ruffing finesse cannot lose. Even if the finesse fails,
you are simultaneously throwing a losing card.

It turns up again and again. All you need to do is recognize it:
       Jx        AK109
You can lead the jack and take an ordinary finesse, or you can play out
the A K and lead the 10 for a ruffing finesse, throwing a losing card.
Which you do depends on which hand you would prefer to lead if you
lose to the queen.

You are beginning to manoeuvre the cards to your own advantage.
With a ruffing finesse you are prepared to throw a losing card on
another losing card. This *loser-on-loser* play comes up in many other
guises.

In the hand which follows it guarantees a contract which might otherwise go wrong:

♠xxxx
♡xx
◇Axx
♣AJ10x

♠AKQJ109
♡Jxx
◇Kxx
♣x

You are in 4♠ and West leads the AKQ of hearts. You can ruff the third one, but look carefully. Your losers are two hearts and a diamond, but there is still a considerable danger that East will overruff the third heart.

Here is where loser-on-loser play comes in. Don't ruff the third heart. Throw a losing diamond from dummy instead. Now the rest of the tricks are yours.

Loser-on-loser play turns up more often than you may think, especially as a means of putting one particular defender on lead. Here we are back to danger hands and safe hands with this unassuming example:

Qxx

Axx

If you play these cards yourself, you can make two tricks only by leading the ace and following with a small card to the queen, hoping for the king on your left. But another suit may provide a loser-on-loser play which throws the lead into the East hand. If East is forced to lead this suit you are guaranteed two tricks, wherever the king lies.

These manoeuvres will come to you with experience. In the meantime, nothing in declarer play is more important than planning, watching how the cards fall, drawing inferences from the defenders' signals and discards, and using ordinary common sense. If one defender has bid, there lie most of the high cards against you. If a defender has doubled, that hand probably has most of your trumps. Think, and play accordingly.

And give the defence every opportunity to make mistakes. If you have a sufficient trump suit, play one or two extra. The defence may have difficulty with discards and throw something that benefits you. Tempt mistakes.

In a perfect world, nobody would make a mistake; but bridge players are alive with imperfections. You will make more hopeless contracts because of bad defence than by any amount of skilled play!

# 12 Tightening up the defence

That was the two of clubs your partner led – a dull, inanimate object, the lowest of its breed. Is that how you see the two of clubs? Or as a lively little fellow bearing an important message from your partner? ('I have either three or four clubs, no more and no less, and I have an honour in this suit. Sorry I cannot be more explicit, but you may be able to make some use of this information.

'Of course there is something else too. My card may be a singleton, but if it is you should have no trouble working that out.')

Now is *that* how you thought about the two of clubs? Or did you bury it in your own indifference?

If you did, you have forgotten the first lesson of defence; that it is all about collaboration between partners, each watching what the other plays and fusing two hands into one.

Defence is difficult. Make it easier for yourself by looking at dummy when it first goes down, assessing whether it is under- or over-strength for its bid. This may help to determine your line of play.

Count dummy's points, assume what declarer has on the bidding and you will have a fair idea of what your partner holds. If it looks like five or six points you will get nowhere by hoping for two aces! But always assume that a contract can be broken, if necessary by 'putting' specific cards in your partner's hand.

In general, you will defend *passively* when dummy has straggly holdings or it seems that declarer has nowhere much to go, *aggressively* if you can see a suit which will provide discards – or a combination of the two.

Look at these two examples:

**1** South opens 1NT and all pass. Your partner leads the *heart* 3:

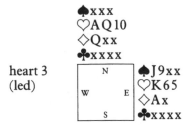

Declarer puts up the ten and you take the king. What sort of a hand is this? Your partner appears to have about 10/11pts including four or five hearts to the jack, and not more than three clubs. (Declarer won't have opened 1NT with a singleton club.)

Don't give your opponent any help at all. Lead a heart back. It doesn't give away a trick which declarer cannot make anyway. When you get in again lead another heart. Play passively and make declarer work for a living.

2  South is in 4♠; your partner leads a trump:

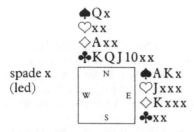

    ♠Qx
    ♡xx
    ◇Axx
    ♣KQJ10xx

spade x
(led)

    N
  W   E
    S

    ♠AKx
    ♡Jxxx
    ◇Kxxx
    ♣xx

This is very different. Your partner, with only two or three points, cannot possibly hold the AK or AQ of hearts to add to your two tricks. You are going to get in once more with the top spade, so now is the only chance you have to do something before all declarer's losers are thrown on the clubs.

If your partner's points are bound up in the *heart* king you have one trick only and no hope. But suppose they are the QJ or Q10 of diamonds, you might just get in two diamond tricks before the clubs are set up. Play aggressively. Lead the *diamond* king, and when you get in again, play another diamond.

When, as a defender, you take the first trick, you often return the suit your partner led; against a no-trump contract you should usually – we are tempted to say nearly always – do so.

But don't become a slave of habit. Check on dummy's strengths and weaknesses before committing yourself to a conventional decision. It is difficult to frame this advice precisely. Perhaps it is best expressed thus: against no-trump contracts, unless you are *almost sure* there is a better alternative, lead back your partner's suit. Failure to do so sours more partnership relationships than anything else in bridge.

If you have convinced yourself that more profit lies in another suit, lead it and avert your eyes from your partner's look of surprise, irritation or fury (none of which should be expressed, but partners are only human). Failure to open up a new suit by blindly returning partner's lead costs many defences their reward.

Now look at two examples. In each case South is in 3NT.

**1**

♠AKx
♡K86
◇xx
♣xxxxx

heart 5
(led)

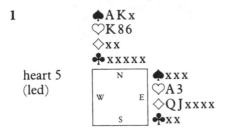

♠xxx
♡A3
◇QJxxxx
♣xx

Dummy plays low and you take the first trick with the *heart* ace. Would you be tempted to lead back a diamond? Most certainly not. Now your ace has gone you have no chance of getting in to make your diamonds. It is true that you might bring off a brilliant *coup* if declarer has precisely Kx and your partner A10x, but now we are back with the idiot boy's dream.

Much more realistically, your partner's hearts may be cleared in one more round. Return your partner's suit.

**2** South again playing in 3NT:

♠K10
♡xxx
◇A103
♣KJ9xx

diamond 4
(led)

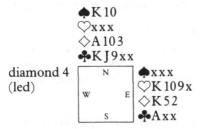

♠xxx
♡K109x
◇K52
♣Axx

Your *diamond* king takes the first trick. Now what? Your partner has led a four-card suit and might take one trick in it. That is of no help. With the clubs as they are and a finesse of the jack (if necessary) succeeding, you are in a hurry. You have the tempo at this moment. Look for three tricks in hearts by 'putting' your partner with the queen. Lead the *heart* 10.

Incidentally, we hope you know by now why your partner must have a four-card suit. The 4 was led, the 3 is in dummy and the 2 is in your hand. Your partner's other cards therefore are *higher* than the 4, so this card, being the fourth highest, is also the lowest of a four-card suit.

Your business in defence is to try to harass the declarer as far as †† possible. One winning way is by forcing declarer to ruff.

Beginners abhor this play, because it means leading high cards which will be trumped ('Oh! but it will be taken!') but look at it the other way round with this hand:

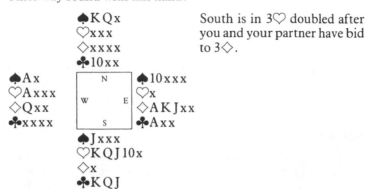

♠KQx
♡xxx
◇xxxx
♣10xx

♠Ax
♡Axxx
◇Qxx
♣xxxx

♠10xxx
♡x
◇AKJxx
♣Axx

♠Jxxx
♡KQJ10x
◇x
♣KQJ

South is in 3♡ doubled after you and your partner have bid to 3◇.

You open a low diamond. Partner takes it and leads another. Declarer ruffs and leads the king of trumps. You take it and lead a third diamond, ruffed again. Now you have three trumps to declarer's two.

When your partner wins with the *club* ace and leads another diamond, the declarer may regret not having taken up tiddlywinks instead of bridge. You have three trumps to declarer's one, *and* the *spade* ace. The hand is in ruins.

Remember our injunction not to be afraid of losing tricks in order to win tricks. This is it with a vengeance.

Your attempt at harassment often consists of doing the opposite of what the declarer is trying to do. If declarer looks like ruffing in dummy, lead a trump so as to begin closing that avenue. Declarer who leads a king before drawing trumps would obviously like you to put your ace on it. Think about it, and perhaps fail to oblige. Declarer leads towards a long suit in dummy headed by the king, this time hoping the ace will not appear. Put it up smartly (second player doesn't always play low) because you sense the lead was a singleton.

If you cannot harass the declarer, at least don't help. When you see that, at some stage, you will either have to cover an honour or not, be ready for it:

```
                A x x
                ┌─────────┐
(you) Q x x     │         │
                └─────────┘
                J (led)
```

Perhaps you have a reason not to cover. Don't sigh and fumble with the queen. Play low smoothly. You don't have to send a telegram to declarer, saying, 'No need to worry, the queen is in my hand.'

## Discarding

Be very careful of discarding from a poor hand. Don't think that what you throw is unimportant. For example, if you see K J x on your right don't cast away all your cards in that suit making it blatantly obvious that the finesse of the jack is bound to succeed.

From a very bad hand be more careful still. A declarer who has found an ace and two kings in your partner's hand will find it difficult to believe that a missing queen is also there. This is an understandable error of thinking, but don't you do anything to correct it.

## More signals

Throwing a high card means, 'Continue the suit.' Throwing a low one may carry the opposite message, 'Lead something else.' For instance:

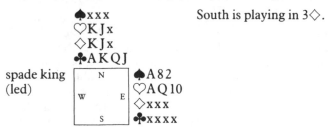

```
        ♠ x x x                    South is playing in 3◇.
        ♡ K J x
        ◇ K J x
        ♣ A K Q J
spade king  ┌──────────┐  ♠ A 8 2
(led)       │  N       │  ♡ A Q 10
            │ W     E  │  ◇ x x x
            │    S     │  ♣ x x x x
            └──────────┘
```

You play the *spade* 2. Far from wanting the suit to be continued, you will only break the contract with a switch to hearts.

Now to the next stage of signalling, the McKenney or suit preference signal. In its elementary form this is when you *lead* a card which indicates to partner which suit you want *led back*. A high card for the higher suit, a low card for the lower one.

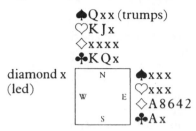

♠Qxx (trumps)
♡KJx
◇xxxx
♣KQx

diamond x
(led)

♠xxx
♡xxx
◇A8642
♣Ax

You read the lead as a singleton, and after winning with the ace will return the suit for a ruff. It is at this moment that you can tell your partner to lead back a club so that you can give a second ruff.

You return the *diamond 2*, your lowest, asking for the low suit. Had you held the *heart* ace you would have returned the diamond 8, asking for the high suit.

Trumps are excluded from the equation, so your partner only has a choice of two suits. In a neat way you are saying which.

The suit preference signal turns up frequently. It is a vital weapon in your defence armoury.

**Opening leads**

The table in Chapter 2 gave the correct lead from every possible holding, except one. That is when you hold the ace of a suit which your partner has bid.

With two cards, Ax, lead the ace. With three or more cards, Axx(x) lead the lowest against a no-trump contract. And against a suit contract? There is a good case for following the rule about unsupported aces and leading another suit. Partner might easily have bid on a suit headed by the queen, so that the cards lie like this:

xxx

Axx          QJ10xx

Kx

However, if you *are* going to lead the suit, the ace is correct – which is why this was omitted from the earlier list. In the early stages, had we even hinted at allowing an unsupported ace to be led, they would all have been led. But you are more experienced now, and you can note this as an exception.

The *choice of suit* for the opening lead when your partner hasn't bid is one that tries the most expert of players. On it may hang the destiny of the game, and that doesn't make it any easier. It is possible to produce a table of the hundred best leads in order of merit, in which case A K Q would be at the top and A Q at the bottom, but this would be extremely misleading. It would take no account of the bidding, which is the crucial factor in choosing the opening lead.

That said, the top of a sequence is obviously a good choice. It fulfils both requirements of an opening lead; it is safe, not giving tricks away, and it is aggressive, setting about taking tricks later.

**The lead against no-trump contracts.** The fourth highest of your longest suit, but the top of a sequence in it if it contains one.

Holding real rubbish, say 10xx Jxxx Jxx xxx, try to lead into your partner's hand with an unbid suit. Spades will do in this instance. Do not lead from your Jxxx in hearts (or in any other suit). You almost invariably give away the only trick you were going to make.

**The lead against a suit contract.** Top of a sequence; top of two touching honours; a singleton – but usually not a singleton of the suit bid on your left, which is unsafe, and generally not a singleton if you have (a) natural trump trick(s) (i.e. KQx, J10xx, etc., when your trumps are more useful to harass the declarer than as ruffs); a doubleton.

Fourth highest of a five-card suit usually turns out safe, of a four-card suit only possibly so.

Leads from Qxx, Jxx, *and top of nothing* (xxx) are moderate, although you have to make them on occasions. Leading from Kxx(x) is generally insecure, but the bidding may help to determine when to make this lead.

Of course your choice of lead is made somewhat easier by excluding all the leads you cannot make, from AQx, KJx, Axx, etc. That will often cut out one or two suits. It may leave you with nothing but a trump to lead, and that is a good choice more often than you may suppose. The opposition bidding is your guide.

Lead a trump:                                                              ††

- if other leads are unsafe;
- often if you have two or three little ones (if you run through your partner's king, never mind, it will be lost anyway);
- if declarer is in a second suit:

$$1\diamondsuit - 1\spadesuit$$
$$2\heartsuit - 3\heartsuit$$

  when ruffing in dummy is declarer's likely play;
- for the same reason, if you think the hand is being played in a 4-4 fit;
- often if the bidding has been strong

$$1\spadesuit - 3\spadesuit$$
$$4\spadesuit$$

  – ruffing may still be the name of the game;
- if you sense a crossruff hand, often one played in 5♣ or 5♢ after other suits have been bid by both opponents – now a trump should leap out of your hand;
- if your partner doubles a low-level contract for penalties – if yours is not the opening lead, lead a trump at the first opportunity;
- if your partner has passed a takeout double, converting it into a penalty.

Do not lead a singleton trump; it may destroy your partner's holding (but ignore this in the last two cases above).

With four trumps, your hope is to force ruffs from the declarer so that control of the hand passes to you. Lead your long suit, breaking a rule if necessary from K J x x x, hoping partner has an honour and you can set about shortening declarer's trumps.

**Leading against slams**
is even more of an imponderable. A general rule is to play passively against a grand slam, usually a trump lead, but to attack a small slam. Against the latter, an ace is a poor lead – that will probably be your only trick. A lead from K x x x or Q x x x may set up a trick in that suit for you to take as well as your ace.

These are merely guidelines. The best of leads can turn out wrong, and the most unlikely may prove brilliant. Attention to the bidding, thoughtfulness, skill and experience combine to decide what you choose. But there is no denying that you also need luck.

# 13 Sundry thoughts on etiquette and other matters

Bridge is fun.

That is why millions of people play it; for entertainment. But you may find it difficult to believe at times. Bridge players have all the failings that the flesh is heir to, and exhibit them rather more than most. They come in every guise: the merry, the morose, the chatty, the taciturn, the ladies and the gentlemen, the bitches and the bastards. They are all playing to enjoy themselves. You must believe that, or you can find no logical reason for their presence at the bridge table.

Perhaps, you say, you should begin playing with friends. You think that is any different? Some of those dear, sweet friends of yours can turn into tyrants when they pick up a pack of cards.

It is an odd game. There is a story from America about a woman who left the bridge table, returned from her bedroom with a gun, and shot her husband dead for calling four hearts. That is possibly a little extreme, but if looks could kill the same sort of thing would be happening every day.

One reason is that about half of all bridge players erroneously believe they play a pretty fair, or even a good, game. They are not so much conceited as knowing; knowing, that is, when and how their partner went wrong, and prepared to say so frankly and fearlessly. The fact that they themselves are often wrong has nothing to do with it. But they are not at heart unpleasant people. They are tender to their husbands and wives, loving to their children and, away from the bridge table, perfectly acceptable company.

We are not trying to put you off. Of course not. We want you to play bridge and play well. This is no more than a gentle warning that once you embark on this strange game you may not find the path suffused with sweetness and light.

Someone once said that you would never lose a friend at bridge if you confined your remarks to 'Well done, partner,' or 'Bad luck, partner.' It isn't easy when your partner has just gone three down in a cast-iron contract, and harder still if he adds, 'I couldn't have got it anyway,' when he could. Then, according to the counsel of perfection, you do not snap out, 'You pot-bellied moron, a child of six could have made that contract!' You say with a smile, 'Bad luck, partner,' and pass on to the next hand.

It isn't easy, but remember, you *are* having fun.

You think these remarks cannot apply to you? That *you* are the one beset with fear of doing the wrong thing? Don't be too sure. Quite early on, you will find that you are better than some of your contemporaries. You would not be human if you did not feel some sense of superiority. Let it stop there. The next stage is to feel, and then express, irritability at a clot of a partner who doesn't appear to know a diamond from a sapphire.

Let it stop before that, because in the next rubber you will be playing with someone better than yourself. Then nothing will dent your morale more easily than a touch of the Genghis Khans across the table. Do as you would be done by. In bridge, as in dancing, your partner is temporarily your soul mate. You won't reprimand a partner on the dance floor who has broken into a tango while you are doing the waltz – and the band is playing rock-and-roll. You'll try to get it together, and so you should at bridge.

And you must not be selfish. One of us still recalls playing a tennis mixed foursome with a buxom girl who constantly swooped to our side of the court and with a scream – 'Mine, partner!' – poached the ball and smashed it into the net. Bridge players do this too:

| | | | |
|---|---|---|---|
| ♠KJxx | 1♡ | ♠Q10xx | 3NT |
| ♡AKJxx | | ♡xx | |
| ◇Jxx | | ◇AKQx | |
| ♣x | | ♣Qxx | |

Three no trumps goes two down, losing five clubs and a spade, but with spades as trumps, eleven tricks are easy. So why did you bid 3NT? We'll be charitable and assume that the 13pts went to your head and you forgot the natural response of 1♠.

But we know plenty of players who bid 3NT on this sort of hand for a less worthy reason. That way they'll be sure to play the hand, whereas if they bid 1♠ there is a good chance, they think, of partner bidding no trumps and becoming the declarer. That sort of partnership is doomed from the start, with each in turn distrusting – or worse still, ignoring – the other.

Partner leads a suit against a no-trump contract. When you get in, lead the same suit back. That shows you trust your partner; and it is always right unless you can see some outstanding alternative. (See Chapter 12)

The dealer opens with 1♠ and your partner overcalls 2♡, which is doubled. This is the overcall we warned you about, the one which can carry a colossal penalty:

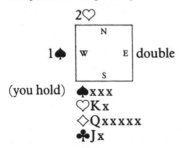

(you hold) ♠xxx
♡Kx
◇Qxxxxx
♣Jx

What are you going to do? Scowl, rescue into 3◇, or what?

Or what is right. Pass. If your partner *has* made a frightful bid, there is one worse: 3◇ from you. And don't scowl, or you'll be made to look an idiot, because your partner held:

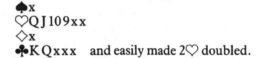

♠x
♡QJ109xx
◇x
♣KQxxx   and easily made 2♡ doubled.

Trust your partner.

You will be unlucky if you meet cheats at bridge; but scowlers, tut-tutters, pitying-lookers and angry remarkers you may, later. They don't really mean any harm. That's their way of enjoying themselves. You see, bridge can grab you. To watch a partner playing a hand all wrong is like watching a friend drive your new car off the road and into a tree. As you survey the wreck, do you say, 'Bad luck, friend'? If so, bully for you, but it is undeniably hard on the nervous system.

The ethics of bridge are quite straightforward, and no more than good manners. Be courteous to your partner and your opponents at all times. Do not indicate by word or gesture the contents of your hand, other than by making a bid.

You may not, for instance, pause for a long time and then pass. That is the same as telling your partner, 'I nearly had a bid.'

Nor should you use different inflections of voice:

One spade – *two* spades (curtly)
One spade – two spa-a-a-ades? (with a rising tone)

The first one says, 'I can just bid two.' The second, 'I can almost bid three.'

Don't complain. It is one thing to have a friendly chat after a hand on how it might have been bid or played (but such inquests should not go on for long because at least one player will be getting bored). It is another to gain the reputation of being a nag. Even if you are right, don't push it. Know-alls are as unpopular as know-nothings.

Don't grumble about what bad cards you hold, and how you haven't picked up a decent hand for a week. It just embarrasses the other players. One of them may make an effort to be sympathetic, but actually nobody cares. If they have any feelings on the subject they will be rather pleased; at least, your opponents will be.

And, anyway, it isn't true that you hold bad cards and have bad luck. People who complain about being unlucky usually aren't. True, they may take three finesses on a hand and lose all three of them, but it wasn't bad luck. They could have made the contract without finessing even once.

The *rules* of bridge will be a mystery to you for a long time to come. There are penalties for revoking, bidding or playing out of turn, and so on. These rules are so convoluted as to be almost impenetrable even to experienced players, so don't worry about them until you need to. When the time comes and a rule is quoted against you, accept gracefully that some misdemeanour of yours will cost you, and your partner, dearly.

Don't get lost among rules and ethics. Which do you suppose it is if a player opens a no trump on 18pts, having declared that the opening no trump is a weak one on 12–14pts? Unruly or unethical?

Actually it is neither (unless the partnership has a secret agreement that, say, no-trump openings become strong at five minutes past each hour – which is cheating). Such a daft opening bid works more against the partner than the opponents, so no code is broken.

Don't give away clues during the play. Neither look as if you are bound on a voyage to paradise, nor as if you are heading for the last roundup. This is for your own sake. However hopeless a contract, set off with a nice confident manner:

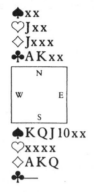

♠xx
♡Jxx
◇Jxxx
♣AKxx

♠KQJ10xx
♡xxxx
◇AKQ
♣—

You are in 4♠ and the ace and another spade are led. You are staring at three or four heart losers, as well as the spade. Of course, if you could get into dummy . . . But don't tell the enemy that you can't.

These are the four hands:

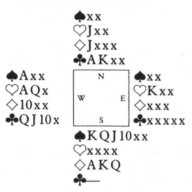

♠xx
♡Jxx
◇Jxxx
♣AKxx

♠Axx          ♠xx
♡AQx          ♡Kxx
◇10xx         ◇xxx
♣QJ10x        ♣xxxxxx

♠KQJ10xx
♡xxxx
◇AKQ
♣—

After the ace and another spade you draw the third trump, then lead the AKQ of diamonds. What now? A low heart towards the jack. West takes it with the queen, hesitates . . . and leads the queen of clubs.

You throw two hearts on the AK of clubs and another on the *diamond* jack.

You couldn't get to dummy, but with a little help you found yourself there.

This hand teaches three lessons. Don't ever give up. Don't wear your heart on your sleeve. Do think positively.

Build up confidence. You can't make a contract, you think. It's impossible. It isn't, and the reason why is that you are playing not against a machine but against two human beings who are as fallible as you. The contract isn't hopeless. Play on and wait for the other side to make mistakes. Your easy air of confidence, hiding a feeling of despair – but *they* don't know that – may cause one of them to crash out an ace in desperation: it was the only way you could succeed.

It would be good for you, from the beginning, to play among your friends for a modest stake: 1p or 2p a 100. That is not gambling. It sharpens you up if you are continually paying for your mistakes by handing over 10p pieces. And it is good for your morale to collect 10p pieces, honourably won.

You are bound to make mistakes, plenty of them. Everybody does. The trick is to learn from each mistake and try not to make the same one again. Soon you will recognize patterns of bidding and cardplay which you can handle. Then you are on your way.

And having fun.

### BIDDING: THE MOST COMMON ERRORS

1 Underbidding, *particularly on the second round*, opener or responder.

*Opener*

1♡ with ♠K10x     response 2♣
      ♡AKJxx
      ◇KQx
      ♣Jx

Rebid *3NT*, not 2♡ or 2NT.

*Responder*

After an opening 1♡, you bid 1♠ with
      ♠AJxx
      ♡xx
      ◇KJ10x
      ♣Axx

(Rebid 2♡)      now 3NT (not 2NT).

2 Opener making wrong rebid.
  1♠ with ♠AKxxx    response 1NT or
      ♡xx        2♣
      ◇Q10xx
      ♣Ax

Rebid 2◇, not 2♠ (do give partner a choice).

3 Responder bidding four-card suits at the two-level, i.e. 1♡–2♣ must have 5 clubs (except in circumstances explained in Part 2).

**4** Responder, when partner rebids a suit, not supporting with 3 trumps.

(Opening 1♡): you bid 1♠ with ♠K J x x x
♡x x x
♢A 10
♣Q x x

(Rebid 2♡)        3♡, not 2NT or 2♠.

**5** Jumping to the conclusion that partner 'doesn't like your suit' simply because he bids something else on the first round. First-round bids are generally exploratory; partner does not hold four cards in your suit, but may have three good ones.

**6** Not opening a weak NT, but choosing a suit instead (usually 1♣ or 1♢). If you are playing a weak NT, play it – except when holding a good five-card major. With a five-card minor, often open 1NT; with a four-card minor, always open 1NT on 12–14pts.

**7** Opener forgetting the rebid of 1NT with 15 or 16pts.

**8** Responder passing on 6 or 7pts, instead of bidding 1NT on hands like this:

(Opening 1♠):   ♠J x x
♡x x
♢K x x x
♣K x x x

Don't think to yourself, 'Oh, I haven't any-thing in hearts,' and pass. Show you have enough points to get into the action with 1NT.

Remember opener has a range of 13–20/21pts, and may only need to hear a squeak from you to bid game.

**9** Overcalling. Making overcalls in a suit when a takeout double would be more flexible. Employ the takeout double whenever you can.

**10** Overcalling with a four-card or weak five-card suit at the two-level. Never do it with a four-card suit, only with a five-card suit which will stand up to pressure. Penalty doubles of poor overcalls can be expensive. When competing for a part score or a rubber, give yourself a little latitude, but still be careful.

11 Doubling. Not doubling for penalties nearly often enough, especially when you hear a bid like the last one:

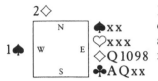

2◇

1♠

♠xx
♡xxx
◇Q1098
♣AQxx

Double. Your partner has opened; you have 3 or 4 tricks and good trumps, and you cannot see a game for your side.

Sometimes, of course, you will have a choice of a game (or possible game) or a double. Add the *heart* king to the above hand, and you could bid 2NT. But still double for penalties. You can always win the next hand!

12 The opposite of number 11 is doubling for penalties too readily when partner has not bid. Unless your double is cast iron and you can see your opponents two down, don't double.

Maybe you have five of their trumps to the queen and an ace outside. Let declarer find out the bad news. Don't double and signpost where the danger lies. But temper this advice with common sense; it would be craven not to double 4♠ with QJ109x in trumps and an outside trick.

### Playing the cards: the most common errors

Not thinking before playing.

### Bidding and playing the cards: the most common errors

Ignoring your partner.

# Part 2
# Becoming more proficient

We have three reasons for writing a Part 2 to this book. The first (remember the inflexible commands of Victorian parents to their children) is to qualify some of the advice given in Part 1. For the sake of clarity and ease of understanding, this advice appeared without reservation. There is nothing wrong in that. However, bridge is not a game which can sustain bald statements of fact. Some of them shout out for a rider, 'But if . . .'

Suppose you were making a first visit to Paris. You read a guide book which says, 'You must not miss Napoleon's tomb, and the best way to visit it is by Metro. Buses tend to be infrequent and slow.' That would be good advice, and you would not be wrong to take it.

But it is not *all* the possible advice. In the first place, many would say that a visit to the Eiffel Tower would be more rewarding; secondly, buses flow freely in off-peak periods; and thirdly, no mention was made of taking a taxi or sauntering off on foot.

In the same sort of way, we stated that if your partner opens 1♠, you respond 4♠ on 13–15pts. That is true if your destination is 4♠, but not if you are aiming at 6♠. Then you need to fish around in other suits; travelling, so to speak, not directly by Metro but by other more devious means.

We said that you should not bid a suit with less than four cards in it. That, too, is true in ordinary circumstances. At other more spacious times you can bid on three, two, one or even no cards in a suit.

So the first reason for Part 2 is to qualify the original advice. The second is to broaden the horizons of your bidding and cardplay.

If you have already played a fair amount, you will surely have encountered hands which seem to admit of no sensible bid. We will give you some new ideas. You will have played contracts which, although correctly bid, have seemed impossible to make. If this was due to bad distribution against you or bad luck, nobody can do anything about that; but some might have been made with different lines of play of which you are yet unaware. We will suggest some of these.

The third reason is quite different. We should like you to stand away from the technicalities of bridge and understand the real fascination of the game. You will be asked to engage in some flights of fancy, some detective work, and some . . . but wait now until the last chapter.

# 14 More bidding

If you lived in some far-off backward place you might reasonably be brought up to think that the mule was the most efficient form of transport. You might continue to believe it all your days, unless a traveller arrived at your door with wondrous tales of the internal combustion engine.

In bridge such a revelation never comes at all to the majority of players, for while Acol is a flexible, evolving system, the teaching of beginners has hardly evolved at all. They are, so to speak, put on muleback while good players are whizzing about in motor cars.

This isn't fair on you, nor is it necessary. When you learn golf or tennis you are not instructed in the first place to hold the club or racket in the wrong way, and then expected to put your grip to rights later. You are taught correctly from the start.

And so you should be. It is as easy to learn well as to learn badly. It is, in fact, much easier to drive a motor car than to ride a mule.

So our purpose in this book has been to set you off with a bidding system which is both simple and expert. It entails, as we warned in the preface, slight modifications to the way in which beginners are traditionally taught.

They come under three headings. One is significant; the other two less so. The minor ones are:

- you need 16pts to double a weak no trump (traditionally 14);
- you need 9 high card points to raise an opening bid of one to two in another suit, e.g. 1♠–2♦ (traditionally 8).

Neither of these needs comment. We assure you they are sensible, and standard bids by any good player.

The significant one is the choice of suit for an opening bid of one. Conventional teaching has it that you open the higher of touching suits of equal length and the lower of non-touching ones. Ours, as you know, is to open the lower of four-card suits, and the higher of five-card suits excepting when you hold clubs and spades.

As far as *five-card suits* of equal length are concerned, most teachers advocate opening the higher, as we do; however, some old books still in print and widely circulated over the years imply that you should open the lower, for instance 1◇ on this:

♠AKxxx
♡xx
◇AKJxx
♣x

If we put in a possible responder's hand you can see what may happen.

|  | | | old-style bidding | opening the higher |
|---|---|---|---|---|
| ♠AKxxx | | ♠xxx | | |
| ♡xx | | ♡AKxxx | 1◇ – 1♡ | 1♠ – 2♡ |
| ◇AKJxx | | ◇xxx | 1♠ – 2NT? | 2♠ – 3♠ |
| ♣x | | ♣KJ | ? | 4♠ |

An easily biddable game replaces a funny old muddle.

Our principal variation involves the opening with two *four-card suits*; one example will make the point clear:

|  | | | old-style bidding | opening the lower |
|---|---|---|---|---|
| ♠AKQx | | ♠xxx | | |
| ♡K10xx | | ♡Axxx | 1♠ – 2NT | 1♡ – 3♡ |
| ◇Kx | | ◇Qxx | 3NT | 4♡ |
| ♣xxx | | ♣KQx | | |

The 4♡ contract should play easily; 3NT will probably fail on a minor suit lead.

The problem with traditional bidding is that there is no distinction in the bidding between:

♠AKxx          ♠AKxxx          Each opens 1♠ and rebids 2♡, but
♡KQxx   and   ♡KQxx          partner cannot know whether the
                                          opposite hand contains four or five
                                          spades.

Our modified openings make this absolutely clear. We open 1♡ on the first of the two above and 1♠ on the second, and this has one clear advantage: *nearly every time we open a suit and rebid a lower one we are showing at least five cards in the opening suit.*

1♠ – 2◇                          1◇ – 1♠
2♡     shows five spades.    2♣     usually shows five diamonds.

Now the responder can safely raise the first suit on only three trumps. Of course, on the hand below, traditionalists will ask the question:

♠AKQx     If your partner responds, say, 2♣, to your 1♡, how are
♡K 10xx   you going to show your spades without overbidding?
◇Kx       You have not the values for a reverse.
♣xxx

The answer is that we don't. If partner doesn't respond a spade we assume no major suit fit and make the natural rebid of 2NT. Every eventuality is covered.

Well, nearly every eventuality. No bidding system yet invented is completely flawless, but we are confident that ours is less flawed than others.

### The opening on three four-card suits

Traditionally you open the suit below the singleton, so:

♠AQxx     Conventional opening is 1♠ (spades are
♡KJxx     treated as below clubs).
◇AJxx     1♠ – 2♣
♣x        2◇ . . . but what happened to the hearts?

We open 1♡, and once again we will find out about a major suit fit on the responder's first bid.

The lynchpins of modern bidding are:

1 the opening weak INT on 12–14pts;
2 the rebid of 1NT on 15 or 16pts;
3 the discovery as early as possible of a fit in a major suit.

Our modified openings concern **3** only. We shall find that fit (or not) more quickly, usually at the one-level. This is a considerable advance.

Furthermore, as we said in the preface, it will not matter in the least if you use our openings and your partner is still bidding in the old style. You will understand each other well enough – and anyway, most partners won't notice the difference.

But you will score heavily if you and your partner are both playing our method.

And, left to the end, again because we open the lower of four-card suits (which can never be 1♠), our opening 1♠ automatically shows a five-card suit.

The only exception is on a 4-3-3-3 hand like this:

| | |
|---|---|
| ♠QJxx | You open 1♠ intending to bid 2NT over 2♣, |
| ♡Kxx | 2◇ or 2♡. However, we strongly recom- |
| ◇AJx | mend opening 1♣ on these hands, so as always |
| ♣Axx | to preserve 1♠ openings for five-card suits. |

As you grow more confident perhaps you will drop a gentle hint that it is time to dismount from the mule and take the wheel of a motor car.

All bidding should be natural. That is what Acol is all about. The following pages go into some detail, but the bidding remains simple and natural. Convoluted bids and tortuous sequences to ram home a single (usually unimportant) point have no place in Acol.

We shall come to one or two speciality bids in a moment. For now let us begin with the obvious (but not always remembered) fact that with a poor hand you will want to stop bidding as early as possible, while with a better one you will encourage, and with a good one you are going to bid game or slam.

Chapter 3 gave you the points necessary for various stages of bidding, and nothing has altered since then. Bid inside your limits, and then use your imagination – and some of the comments which follow – to test the water. Be sensible, but not pedantic.

The opening bid and the first response are simple. They don't often admit of a choice, and if they do the correct choice is not difficult to make.

Second-round bids are different. A separate book could be written about opener's and responder's second and third bids, and subtle ways of expressing strength or weakness, length or shortage. We have no space for such a catalogue. Instead we shall add some cosmetic touches and a few new practical ideas to your existing bidding.

First, though, a generality. Try not to think of your hand, and the points it contains, as a fixed star around which the planets of your partner and the opponents circulate. By now you should know that it is no such thing. It is subject to numerous influences, particularly your partner's delight or despair.

For example:

| | |
|---|---|
| ♠KQJ10xx | You open 1♠ and your partner responds 2♣. |
| ♡— | You are certainly going to make a game, and |
| ◇AQxx | perhaps a slam. |
| ♣xxx | *But:* |
| | You open 1♠, and your partner responds 2♡. |
| | Game is only probable; by no means certain. |

And again:

| | |
|---|---|
| ♠Qxxx | You open 1◇ and the response is 1♠. Distri- |
| ♡A | bution and fit are all on your side. Forget the |
| ◇AQJxxx | points and bid 4♠. |
| ♣xx | *But:* |
| | You open 1◇ and the response is 1♡. Now all |
| | you are worth is a rebid of 1♠. |

An understanding of the value of 'shape' will guide you to rebid correctly on many hands. However, students of point-counts may get close to the same result in another way. Opener's hand has included no points for shortages; if responder becomes the declarer, opener's singletons and doubletons take on a new value and can be added to the point count. The choices, of course, are not always as easy as these.

| | |
|---|---|
| ♠xx | You open 1♡, and the response is 2◇. You |
| ♡AKJxx | are just worth a rebid of 3♣. Change the *heart* |
| ◇Kx | king for the *heart* queen, and 2♡ would be |
| ♣AJ10x | enough. |

| | |
|---|---|
| ♠AKQJ10x | You open 1♠ and the response is 2NT. With |
| ♡Q10 | such a strong spade suit and good inter- |
| ◇J109 | mediates, a pass would be cowardly. A rebid of |
| ♣xx | 3♠ might be passed; 4♠ is too much. 3NT is |
| | the sensible course. Your spades will take |
| | tricks in no trumps too. |

Now for some detail:

*Opener*

On many hands you have a choice of rebids:

♠Kx
♡AK10xx    Opening 1♡ – response 1♠.
◇Qxxx
♣Ax

†† You have three choices of rebid: 2◇, 1NT or 2♡. On all ordinary hands this is the order of priority:

**1** bid a second suit;

**2** bid 1NT, with 15/16pts;

**3** rebid your suit.

So on this hand your bid is 2◇. Without four diamonds you choose 1NT, and only if neither is available do you rebid your suit.

*Responder*

† **1** You almost always support your partner's four-card major suit opening with four cards or more in it, but there is no such obligation to support a minor suit. You sometimes have to make responses of 1♣–3♣ or 1◇–3◇, but they are usually unsatisfactory, leaving the opener with the problem of bidding a risky 3NT, or 5♣ or 5◇ with possibly inadequate values.

    If you can, bid another suit first, with a possible 3NT in mind; you can always fall back into 3♣ or 3◇ later.

**2** Remember, holding two four-card major suits, bid hearts first or you may miss a fit. Shade the values for the response in a major suit to any xxxx.

**3** With two five-card major suits, bid the higher first.

**4** A response of 1NT facing an opening 1♣ shows 8pts at least. With, for instance, xxx Qxx Qxxx Kxx, respond 1◇.

† Many players nourish the belief that 1NT is the weakest response. It isn't. It is exactly the same – 6–10pts – and, facing 1♣, sometimes stronger.

**5** With 10pts it is usual to underbid, unless holding a good fit with partner or good intermediates:

Reply 1NT on: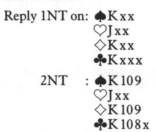
♠Kxx
♡Jxx
◇Kxx
♣Kxxx

2NT : ♠K109
♡Jxx
◇K109
♣K108x

For a further alternative with 10pt hands see p.162.

**6** On quite a few hands it is preferable to show a four-card major to a poor five-card minor.

(Opening 1♡): with  ♠KJ10x
♡x
◇Jxxxx
♣Axx

1♠ is a better response than 2◇.

**7** Sometimes it is politic to support partner's opening with three cards in the suit. For obvious reasons this has been left until Part 2, for once beginners are allowed this latitude they seize on it and reply with three trumps, or even two, with merry abandon.

In all ordinary circumstances you still need four trumps to support. With three you may end in a 4-3 fit, which is not a consummation devoutly to be wished. However, bridge is a flexible game in all its aspects. Given a choice of two inferior bids, break a rule and choose the less inferior.

For example:

(Opening 1♠):                    with ♠QJx
                                      ♡x
                                      ◇Jxxxx
                                      ♣Qxxx

2♠ is far superior to 1NT.

But confine such bids to occasions when:

● you hold a trump honour;
● you are weak, 6–10pts; and, sometimes
● if 2♠ gives you game.

*Opener*

The same flexibility applies to you. On suitable hands you can support partner with only
three cards.

   For example:

♠AQx    The bidding so far has gone
♡xxxxx  1♡–1♠ (an opening 1NT would
◇KQx    have been better; however . . .).
♣Kx

We have said that all five-card suits are rebiddable. They are, and on this hand a rebid of
2♡ follows the rule book; however, the hearts
are pitiful, and you should try to look elsewhere.

   1NT is possible, but a point short, and you
should avoid deceit if you can on the very
precise point count required in no-trump
bidding.

   2♠ is much the best choice.

**Trial bids**
There is no such bidding as:

            1♠ – 2♠
            3♠ – 4♠

Neither partner has enough knowledge of
what the other holds, and both are being
pressurized to overbid.

After 1♠ – 2♠, opener – with about 17pts – should bid the suit in which help is wanted.

♠A K J x x
♡A x
♢Q x x x
♣K x         rebid 3♢.

*Responder*

Bid 4♠ with 9 or 10pts, and also with less if you have a high honour or a shortage in diamonds.
Otherwise, sign off with 3♠.

## Opening light

It will usually pay to open the bidding with less than 13pts, if your bid can be justified. This is particularly true third in hand, after two passes.

The general principle of opening light is that the high cards in your hand must relate to the longer suits. For example, you may open 1♠ on:

♠A Q x x x
♡K J 10 x
♢x x
♣x x

But not on: ♠x x x x x
♡A K
♢x x x
♣A x x

Not only is the first hand more secure but also, if the opponents gain the contract, you will welcome a spade lead. On the second, a spade lead may destroy the defence.

## Biddable suits
Shade them if necessary down to Jxxx, but
only in the minors. You may open 1◇ on:

    ♠AQxx
    ♡Ax
    ◇Jxxx
    ♣Axx

## Hand valuation

Right back in Chapter 1 we told you to pass a single-raise limit bid
with 13–16pts. That still goes for ordinary hands, but as a statement it
is much too all-embracing.

Look at the difference between these two hands after the bidding
1♠–2♠:

♠AKJxxx   and  ♠AKJxxx
♡x                ♡xx
◇AJ10x        ◇AJx
♣xx              ♣xx

Each contains 15pts, including distribution, but otherwise how different they are. The first has a 6-1-4-2 distribution and a strong
intermediate card in the diamond 10. It is nearly, but not quite, worth
an immediate rebid of 4♠. Make a trial bid of 3♣ as described earlier.
The second hand has no quality other than the six-card suit. You
should pass 2♠.

Hand valuation is too long and tricky a subject to enter into here.
Meanwhile your eyes will be your guide; you probably saw how
superior the first hand was to the second, without comment from us.

## Opening on 21 or 22pts

*a*  2NT, of course, with a balanced hand.
*b*  A strong two with eight playing tricks, but
    not on scattered values – you would already
    be telling the sort of lie which leads to
    misunderstanding.
*c*  Otherwise, with 21 or 22pts you must either
    grit your teeth and open one of a suit, or tell
    a fairly white lie and open 2♣. It depends
    on how little you need for game and how

much your partner's response is likely to
help. For example:

♠AKQxx        Open 2♣. With minimal help
♡Axx          you should make a game.
◇AKJx
♣x

But:

♠K            Open 1♣. If your partner
♡AQJx         passes, you probably haven't
◇AQx          missed game.
♣KQxxx

## More on reverses

You are not strictly reversing if the *opponents*
force you to bid higher than you intended. For
instance:

　　　　1♣　1♠　2◇　no bid
　　　　2♡

But for the intervention you would have bid
1♡ over 1◇. To bid 2♡ now you need to be
no better than minimum.

### Flexibility by responder

We have stressed the need to hold a five-card
suit when responding at the two-level: for
instance, 1♠ – 2♣ shows five clubs. Adhere to
this when your hand is worth only one bid,
with 9 or a poor 10pts. But there are numerous
exceptions. You may reply with less than a
five-card suit under the following conditions:

1 You have 16pts or more, when you force to
   show your points.

2 You have sufficient points for game, but no
   evidence yet of what the contract will be:

   (Opening 1♠):  ♠Jxx
   　　　　　　　　♡AQxx
   　　　　　　　　◇xx
   　　　　　　　　♣AKxx

Bid 2♣, and see what happens next.

**3** You do know what the contract will be, but want to keep your options open in case of a slam, then the *delayed game raise*:

(Opening 1♠):  ♠AJxx
           ♡x
           ♦AKQxx
           ♣xxx

Bid 2♦, and after opener's rebid, bid 4♠.

This bid shows 13–15pts and ideally suggests the values are in two suits, your own and your partner's, as in the example. Sometimes, however, you will have to give a delayed game raise with a slightly different holding.

It follows that direct jumps to game in opener's suit, 1♠–4♠, are reserved for distributional hands such as:

           ♠KJxxx
           ♡x
           ♦KQxxx
           ♣xx

**4** You are strong enough for another bid, but not necessarily for game, and would like to hear more before making up your mind:

(Opening 1♠):  ♠10xx
           ♡AJxx
           ♦xx
           ♣AQxx

Bid 2♣. You can look after any reply from opener: after 2♠–3♠; after 2♦–2NT; after 2♡–3♡; after 3♣–pass.

**5** Under this heading comes responses on 10pt hands on which after an opening, say of 1♠ you would like to bid 2½♠ or 1½NT, but you can't. Best, if you can, to temporize with 2♣ or 2♦ as on the above 11pt hands; after your partner's reply, you may know better whether to pass or continue.

**6** You have nothing except a long, strong minor suit.

(Opening 1♠): ♠xx
♡x
♢xxxx
♣AQJxxx

Bid 2♣, then 3♣ over opener's rebid.

Here we will cast some light on the differences between the major and the minor suits. Because 4♡ and 4♠ are by far the most common suit contracts in the game, the majors have a solid, almost severe, countenance. They are not to be trifled with. But clubs and diamonds are more frivolous. You can introduce them, so to speak, *en passant*, without much fear that your partner will leap to 5♣ or 5♢. You can play little games with the clubs and diamonds; bidding sometimes only two- or three-card suits, making them work for you and using them as holding bids in order to gain time and information from your partner.

In all sequences such as those above, your 2♣ or 2♢ are opening the way to other bids. You should never use the majors in the same context, or you may find yourself hurtled into 4♠ or even 6♠ before you can draw breath.

### No-trump bidding, a warning note

Other than the all-purpose and limited 1NT responses by opener or responder, bids in no trumps are made on positive grounds, because the bidding suggests the hand will play better in no trumps than in a suit. They are *not* bids made because there is no fit in a suit.

Contract after contract fails because, 'I don't like your suit and you †† don't like mine, so we'll play in no trumps.' This sort of thing:

| ♠x | ♠KQxx | |
|---|---|---|
| ♡AKxxxx | ♡Jx | Bidding: 1♡–1♠ |
| ♢Jx | ♢Axxxx | 2♣ |
| ♣AQxx | ♣xx | |

Now you must keep out of no trumps. The next bid should be 2♡, not 2♢ or 2NT. And if 2♢ is bid by some careless responder, opener should most certainly rebid 2♡, not 2NT.

And again:

♠x                 ♠K 10 x x x
♡A K x x x x       ♡x                    Bidding: 1♡ – 1♠
◇A K x x           ◇x x x                          2◇
♣x x               ♣A J x x

Full marks now for a pass by responder. Misfits should be played at as low a level as possible. 3NTs on such hands is a graveyard in which many partnerships come to rest.

††    Hands that do not fit in a suit do not often fit in no trumps.

There is another point about such hands. More often than you would like you hold a singleton in partner's suit. There is nothing you can do about it, short of plucking a card from your sleeve. It is not your fault, nor is it the end of the world. Don't writhe in search of a bid. Realize that the hands do not fit and try to stop at a low level before you go over the precipice. Let your partner play the hand. Singleton or not, the part-score contract will often be made. And if it fails, it is a fair bet that there was nowhere better to go, certainly not to no trumps.

That said, a singleton holding is not an absolute bar to a 3NT contract, so long as you assess it on positive grounds and not as a bolt-hole. For example:

1♡ – 1♠     ♠K Q x x x     Bid 3NTs. There is no point in anything
2♣          ♡x             else, and you may get a diamond lead!
            ◇A Q 10 x x
            ♣Q x

## Fourth-suit forcing

### *Responder*

We are dealing now with one of those occasions when you feel stuck for another bid. We promised to get you out of it, and we will.

Most of the time, after three bids, you will know where the final contract will come to rest, but there can be situations in which the complete picture has not been unveiled.

Bidding: 1♠ – 2♣
      2♡      you hold: ♠A x
                        ♡A x x
                        ◇Q x x
                        ♣K J x x x

The best contract could be 3NT, 4♡, 4♠ or even 5♣. You want more information.

Bid 3◇. The bid of the fourth suit asks opener for clarification, with an accent on bidding 3NT if holding a stop in the fourth suit; if not that, any other clarification, such as a five-card heart suit or support for your suit.

*Opener's reply*

It will be easiest to look at three possible hands, in which the bidding has gone as above:

      1♠ – 2♣
      2♡ – 3◇

**a** ♠KQJ10x  **b** ♠J10xxx  **c** ♠Q10xxx
   ♡KJxx       ♡KJxx      ♡KJxxx
   ◇xx         ◇A10       ◇x
   ♣Qx         ♣A10       ♣A10

On **a** opener replies 3♠, on **b** 3NT and on **c** 3♡.

Responder will raise 3♠ to 4♠ and 3♡ to 4♡.

Bids of the fourth suit at the *three*-level must always be on hands with enough values for game.
    Below the three-level:

      1◇ – 1♠
      2♣ – 2♡

game should at least be a prospect; so a bid of the fourth suit is never made on weakness.
    (And on the above sequence don't worry if you have a two-suiter in spade and hearts; you can make that clear on the next round.)

Opener can bid fourth-suit forcing, but it arises much less often.

## Bidding to a part score

With a part score it is only too easy to settle for a game, without investigating a slam. If you have a fairish hand and a good fit with your partner, don't hesitate to give a gentle push:

♠AQxx
♡KQx
◇KJxx
♣Kx

♠KJx
♡Ax
◇A10xxxx
♣Qx

Score: North-South 60 towards game.

North opens 1♠ and South responds 2◇. If you aren't alert this is where the contract will rest. North should certainly bid 3◇. It can do no possible harm, and in this case will lead to 6◇.

## A useful comparison

Look at these two bidding sequences:

1♡ – 2NT   and   1♡ – 1♠
3♡                 2NT – 3♡

In the first one the opener is saying, 'From my point of view 3NT is going to be full of holes; 3♡ looks like the right spot.' Any responder who now bids 3NT must shoulder all the blame.

Opener may hold something like:

♠xx
♡AKJxxx
◇Kxx
♣xx

The second is totally different. Responder's 3♡ bid is forcing, announcing, 'I have values for game and three hearts. If you have five it may play better in 4♡. Now you make the final bid.'

Responder will hold something like:

♠ A J x x x
♡ Q x x
♢ A Q x
♣ x x

## A new forcing bid

The bidding in Chapter 3 was kept as simple as possible, which is the reason for these notes. This last one involves one of the simplest bidding sequences of all:

1♡ – 1♠ or 2♣
2♢

Opener has, say:

♠ x x
♡ A Q 10 x x
♢ A Q x x
♣ K x

This, you remember, qualifies as a minimum rebid which the responder can either leave or correct to 2♡.

That is true of the response of 1♠; if responder has no further bid to make game is unlikely. But if the response was 2♣ (showing 9pts at least) the two hands are already almost at game-level.

It follows that when the response is at the two-level, the sequence, say, of:

1♠ – 2♢
2♡

the opener's rebid must not be passed; it is forcing for one round.

## Warning

All the bids in this chapter are standard among good players, and you can safely use them with partners you know. They are not fancy or even particularly advanced bids, although they may appear so to players who have never heard of them!

# 15   Overcalling and competing

We dealt fully in Part 1 with the dangerous overcalls of two over one. Nothing has changed. Without the values, without enough tricks in your hand, they are just as dangerous in Part 2, and beyond. Continue to be wary.

One overcall was left without explanation; that is, one over one non-vulnerable, such as:

    1◇

     1♠

which was described as 'unimportant'. This needs further elaboration.

Of course you need some values, but don't be paralysed by the thought that 13pts are a magic minimum. They aren't. For a number of reasons, you want to get into the bidding if you can:

**1** because you have sufficient to get into the bidding:

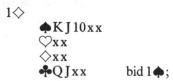

    1◇

     ♠K J 10 x x
     ♡x x
     ◇x x
     ♣Q J x x    bid 1♠;

**2** to harass the opponents; on the hand above you have shut out a response of 1♡;

**3** to try to head the opponents away from a 3NT contract:

    1♣

     ♠Q x x
     ♡x x x x
     ◇A K J x
     ♣x x    bid 1◇;

**4** to attract a sensible lead against any contract; on the above hand you will welcome a diamond lead.

† Because light overcalls are sensible for various reasons, partner should be wary and initially treat them with discretion:

| W | N | E | S |
|---|---|---|---|
| 1♣ | 1♠ | no bid | ? |

♠xx
♡Axxx
◇Qxxx
♣AJx

1NT is quite enough. Await developments: partner will bid again if strong enough.

A jump to 2NT in these circumstances requires 13 or 14pts; to 3NT, at least 15.

When your partner makes any overcall – one over one, two over one, vulnerable or non-vulnerable – you must judge your action in the light of the bidding so far. Once again, tricks should be your guide rather than points.

Your cards may be positioned so that they are of obvious value, or of no value at all:

| W | N | E | S |
|---|---|---|---|
| 1♣ | 1♡ | 1♠ | ? |

♠xx
♡Qxxx
◇KQx
♣KJxx

That looks like 12pts, including one for the doubleton spade, but the values are much less. You can forget about the KJxx in clubs; they are probably worthless. And if your partner has a spade honour, that is of no use either. A raise to 2♡ is enough.

| W | N | E | S |
|---|---|---|---|
| 1♣ | 1♡ | 1♠ | ? |

♠KJx
♡Qxxx
◇KQ
♣xxxx

Now this is a splendid 12pts. With the spade bid on your right, the KJx in your hand are probably working for you, and your partner may be sitting with a club trick over the opener – or a shortage. Bid 3♡ this time.

From these two examples you can see that points do not necessarily translate into tricks. They are your guide to bidding, not your shackles.

An overcall of 1NT is a strong bid. Play it with 15-17 non-vulnerable and 16-18 vulnerable. But 1NT called in fourth position is weak:

| W | N | E | S |
|---|---|---|---|
| 1♡ | no bid | no bid | 1NT |

about 10–14pts

With a better hand, you should bid a suit or double for takeout. This weak bid comes in because you and your partner probably have the balance of the points. You are bidding partly on your partner's hand, and expect to play in a part score.

## Overcalling the opponent's suit

An immediate overcall

> 1♡
>
>      2♡

shows a powerful two-suit hand and replaces a double for takeout; but whereas a double is forcing for only one round, this bid forces to game.

To make such a bid, your hand should be as strong as this:

♠AKQ9xx
♡x
♢AK109x
♣x

As partner of the direct overcaller you must value your hand in the light of the bidding. Suppose the bidding on the hand above goes like this:

| W | N | E | S |
|---|---|---|---|
| 1♡ | 2♡ | no bid | 3♣ |
| no bid | 3♠ | no bid | ? |

♠J10x
♡Axx
♢QJx
♣10xxx

You should realize that your 8pts have grown enormously in stature. Your partner's two-suiter is in spades and diamonds; you have trump support and invaluable diamonds. You should bid vigorously, thinking of a slam.

To overcall opponent's suit you must have a big two-suiter. This is not strong enough:

♠KJ10xxx
♡—
◇—
♣KQxxxxx

In such a case, use your imagination and approach with guile. Bid 2♣. Somebody will bid again, we promise you!

With a three-suit hand, however strong, you must double for takeout.

## Overcalling opponent's suit in the course of the bidding

This is a most useful bid, and another which comes in handy when you are stuck for what to say next. Roughly, it means, 'I have another bid, but it will be easier to make if you clarify your hand.'

Here is a sequence: your partner opens 1♠ and you hold:

♠Qx
♡Axx
◇KJ10xx
♣Kxx

The bidding goes:

| W | N | E | S |
|---|---|---|---|
| 1♠ | 2♣ | 2◇ | no bid |
| 2♡ | no bid | ? | |

Bid 3♣. According to what your partner bids next, the final contract will be 3NT, 4♡, 4♠ or even 5◇.

In this example, the bid of 3♣ – an overcall of opponent's suit at the three-level – is forcing to game. At a lower level it need not be:

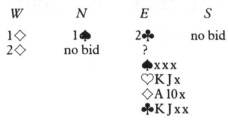

| W | N | E | S |
|---|---|---|---|
| 1◇ | 1♠ | 2♣ | no bid |
| 2◇ | no bid | ? | |

♠xxx
♡KJx
◇A10x
♣KJxx

Bid 2♠. You are searching for a game contract, but can pass a disappointing rebid of 3◇ by opener.

If all this seems a little advanced, here is a suggestion: the next time you know you have a bid and can't think what on earth to say, try to remember either **1** fourth-suit forcing (described earlier), or **2** this overcall. One of them may exactly fit the bill. But a word of warning. Don't tie yourself into unnecessary knots. If you have a natural bid, make it.

## A different overcall of opponent's suit

Sometimes, when one partner has doubled for takeout, the other may deem it better for the doubler to bid the suit. It is done in this way:

| W | N | E | S |
|---|---|---|---|
| 1◇ | double | no bid | 2◇ |

You may hold, as South, something like:

♠K10xx
♡K10xx
◇xx
♣AJx

Your 2◇ bid means, 'I think the best fit will be found if you name the suit.'

## More doubling for takeout

There is no reason why you should not double for takeout on a two-suiter, as long as your missing suit is the low one – but not when it is hearts or spades.

This is even easier if the opponents have bid two suits themselves:

| W | N | E | S |
|---|---|---|---|
| 1◇ | no bid | 1♠ | double |

A double now shows both the unbid suits.

With hands like this:

first double for takeout and then bid 3♡. This shows a stronger hand than an immediate overcall of 3♡.

If your hearts were a little weaker, say AJ9xxx, you would still have the values to call 3♡ over 1♠, but it would place too much stress on your trump suit. Double, then rebid 2♡.

## A question answered

The bidding goes:

A frequent source of confusion arises as to whether the 3♣ bid is forcing or not. The answer is no. The fourth-in-hand bidder has not voluntarily bid at this level, but has been pushed to it.

## The unusual 2NT

A conventional bid, the darling of some players, but a seductive toy to be handled with discretion. After an opening of a major suit, an overcall of 2NT promises a good hand in the minor suits. Game may or may not be makeable in 5♣ or 5◇; if not, the bid prepares the way for a cheap sacrifice at this level over 4♡ or 4♠.

A *cheap* sacrifice. To bid the unusual 2NT, over a one- or two-bid, you must have at least ten cards in the minor suits and not less than five of each, as well as a hand strong in playing tricks with a minimum of about x  xx  KQJxx  AQJ10x.

Partner *must* reply in a minor suit; for example, with x  KJxxxxx  xxx  xx, the response is 3◇.

Many players will have nothing whatever to do with the unusual 2NT, and we know why. It is because they have encountered the bright sparks who shade the bid downwards and ever downwards. The 'unusual' has been heard on x  xx  Jxxxx  Jxxxx. A massacre awaits.

## Competing

If it is at all realistic, it is always worth competing for a part score; 50 or 100 down is a much superior result to 60 below the line to the opponents.

With both sides non-vulnerable, don't worry about going down 300 to save the first game, and 500 is not a disaster. With your opponents a game up it is not worth while; they are odds on to win the rubber. Desperation bidding at this time (mistakenly favoured by most average players) simply piles up a bigger adverse score.

At game all (perhaps this is a matter of taste) 500 down is acceptable.

The situation is more difficult to assess when your opponents have a part score and have opened the bidding. You don't want the game to go too easily, so if you can, you push – but within strict safety limits. Don't underestimate the handicap of fighting against the opponents' part score; their bids of 1◇–2◇ can hide a huge hand of up to 30pts. They have the edge and can double your unwary contract and still retain their 60 below.

Less understood is the need to protect your own part score. It is of such value that you should bid just as vigorously to keep it as you do when trying to drive the opponents too high.

†† None of this is a licence to make stupid bids. Our old favourite, the two-overcall after an opening one of suit, must still be based on a sound five-card suit at least, and the values to ensure at least five tricks. That penalty of 1100 is even more likely to be incurred when you are so obviously competing on nothing.

That said, bid if you can. The opponents are 60 below and on your right a diamond is bid. With K 109x xx xxx AQxx, overcall 1♠. If you don't, you surely cannot wait until the next round and bid 2♠.

The merit of this hand is the spade suit. Spades are the emperor of all the suits, always standing you one ahead of the opposition. If no side holds spades, hearts fulfil the same purpose.

Otherwise, make profuse use of the takeout double in competitive bidding. Over 1♠, double holding x K 10xx AQxxx Qxx. The outcome is anyone's guess, but at least you have resisted the temptation to lay your head on the block with an overcall of 2◇.

In assessing your hand, pay particular attention to the intermediates. 10s and 9s are jewels compared to the dross of 2s and 3s.

There is a psychology attached to competitive bidding. Suppose the opponents with a part score open 1♣, and the bidding continues 2♡, 2♠, 3♡. The opener may suspect you of pushing without sufficient values, but holding no strong hearts is likely to bid 3♠ rather than take what appears to be a small penalty.

At this point your intervention has probably run its course, so beware. Your overcall was only just possible, and your partner may have supported with minimum values. Whereas a bid of 3♡ might not have been penalized, 4♡ will almost certainly attract a double. Give up now.

But suppose your partner does go on to 4♡, and your opponents bid 4♠. You have another weapon in your armoury, a double. It says, 'Partner, I believe they have overstepped the mark, and I feel sure *we* will if we go higher.' It may cost a bit if they make 4♠, but nothing like as much as it will cost our side if partner bids 5♡. There is an old saying: let the other side play at the five-level. Like all old sayings, it has more than a grain of truth in it.

To end, when you are in there fighting, try to bid as you usually do. If you need to pause, let it sound as though you are reflecting on the choice between an admirable suit and no trumps. Don't allow doubts and fears to creep into your behaviour. Perhaps you are going to be doubled, perhaps not. There is no point in *inviting* a double by sounding hopeless about the whole thing.

# 16   No-trump bidding

**The Stayman convention**

Stayman is so widely played that it might have been introduced in Part
1. The principle of it is that, although the opening bid was in no
trumps, the hand may play better in a major suit provided both
partners have four of it. It leads to many successful contracts in 4♡ or
4♠ which would fail in 3NT.

That may seem obvious: if you hold eight trumps between you, a
suit contract is usually preferable to one in no trumps. However, you
will meet many players who do not employ Stayman. Among them
will be those who learned bridge before the convention was invented
(about thirty years ago) and see no need for new-fangled ideas. Many
more know of Stayman but regard it as a rather difficult optional
extra. It is as though when they first discovered how to make a fruit pie
they couldn't be bothered to go out and buy some cream, so that ever
afterwards their pies have had a dry, incomplete presentation.

In fact, Stayman is easy to understand and very profitable to use,
both on strong hands and weak hands.

(Opening 1NT –       Responder, having a positive response and a
weak or strong):      hand which includes a four-card major suit,
                      bids a conventional 2♣, e.g.:

(1NT, weak):   ♠Qxxx
               ♡xx
               ◇AKJx
               ♣Qxx        response 2♣.

Opener replies 2♡ or 2♠ if holding four of
either, otherwise bids a conventional 2◇.

Responder: if opener bids your suit, go to
game, in this case 4♠.

If not, revert to no trumps at the correct
level, in this case 2NT.

Opener will raise 2NT to 3NT with a maximum as usual.

Opener with four cards in both majors bids
2♡ first, and after a no-trump reply shows
spades, i.e.:

  1NT – 2♣
  2♡ – 3NT
  4♠

Stayman is also used in the same way over
2NT openings. Response 3♣.

And on weak hands:

  ♠Jxxxx
  ♡Jxxx
  ◇xxx
  ♣x

You can make a weak takeout into 2♠, but the
hand should play better in 2♡ if your partner
has four of them.

After an opening 1NT, bid 2♣. To a reply
of 2♡, pass. To 2◇, bid 2♠.

Reduced down to one sentence, all Stayman amounts to is an artificial
bid of 2♣ by responder, either 2♡, 2♠ or an artificial reply of 2◇ by
opener, and a resultant contract in a major suit or no trumps.

You need it to complete your no-trump bidding, but with one †
*caveat*: leave out Stayman on flat hands with 4-3-3-3 distribution,
which are likely to play better in no trumps.

Now for some general notes on no-trump bidding. In Part 1 we stressed that you should
choose to open 1NT on all balanced hands,
and on many containing a five-card minor suit,
but that you should open 1♡ or 1♠ with a
five-card major. Sometimes, however, if the
major suit is threadbare, 1NT will be the
better opening bid, for example on:

  ♠Q10
  ♡Jxxxx
  ◇AQx
  ♣Axx

*Responder*

With a good 11pts or more, and a five- or six-card major suit you bid 3♡ or 3♠. With a strong six-carder and no slam in view, jump to 4♡ or 4♠.

You should not be thinking of a slam in a suit with less than 17pts; in NTs with less than 19pts.

With a good 11pts or 12pts and a five-card minor, bid 2NT; but with a strong five-card or six-card minor, jump to 3NT:

♠xx
♡Qx
♢AQ10xxx
♣Axx

Hands like this often make 3NT or 4NT, or go down in 2NT. You might as well be in game.

With 13 or 14pts, and a five-card minor, bid 3NT.

With the values to play in 5♣ or 5♢, reply 3♣ or 3♢; leaving opener the option of the final bid.

†   The values for the jump to three in a minor are a six-card suit, or a strong five-card one, and at least 16pts.

However, with a balanced distribution of 3-5-5-2 bid 3NT unless you are contemplating a slam with 17pts or more.

Slam tries and slam bids facing no-trump openings:

(Opening 1NT weak): with 19–20pts
                                          bid 4NT;
                                          with 21–24pts
                                          bid 6NT.
(three points less facing a strong no trump).

(Opening 2NT):    with 11–12pts
bid 4NT;
with 13–16pts
bid 6NT.

Opener: after a 4NT response, bid 6NT when holding a maximum opening bid; 14pts for 1NT, 22pts for 2NT; otherwise pass.

Acute observers may have noticed that when playing a weak no trump it is possible to land in a game of 4♡ or 4♠ with fewer than the required points. In competition bridge there is a way out of this. In rubber bridge you will be unlucky if both opener and responder have a minimum, but even then there may be a play for game.

Anyway, this will not happen to you so often if you accept that responder must have a minimum of a *good* 11pts to reply. Most teaching says that 11pts are enough; we stress that you should pass 11pt hands which have no quality other than the points.

As for those players who take a merry gamble with a response on 9 or 10pts, just hope they are playing *against* you. They are heading for almost certain doom.

# 17 Strong bids

It is a cardinal error of average players to bid good hands too strongly and poor hands too weakly, if at all. This is particularly relevant to sequences following 2♣ or strong two openings, and slam bidding in general.

Such over- and underbidding is quite understandable, in a way. You so infrequently pick up 24pts that, when you do, you begin to think along the lines of 'all this and heaven, too'. You so often hold bad hands that you are used to letting the bidding fade away and stop.

The error arises, of course, through over-concentration on one's own cards and insufficient projection into partner's hand. It is not, we promise you, confined to beginners.

So we hear ridiculous bidding like:

$$1\diamondsuit - 1\heartsuit \atop 1\spadesuit - 4\text{NT}} \quad or \quad {2\clubsuit - 2\heartsuit \atop 2\spadesuit - 4\text{NT}}$$

As we have said before and will keep on saying, there is *no hurry*. In both these cases there is time and space for at least two more bids; they should be used to explore in general, and in particular to decide whether a Blackwood 4NT is at all justifiable.

Absurd leaps like these frequently lead to a slam in which the A K of one suit is missing, and two quick tricks are lost.

More about Blackwood and the alternative to it comes at the end of this chapter; meanwhile we have some further comments on jump bids.

### Responder's replies to strong openings

We have stressed that responder needs 1½ quick tricks to reply positively to an opening 2♣ or Acol Two. However, modern practice is to shade this somewhat, provided the hand contains a good suit.

(Opening 2♣
2◇, or 2♡):  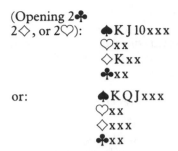  ♠KJ10xxx
♡xx
◇Kxx
♣xx

or:  ♠KQJxxx
♡xx
◇xxx
♣xx

It is too strait-laced to insist on 1½ quick tricks when you hold hands like these. Respond 2♠ in each case. But note that it is the strength of the suit which is the justification.

## Jump bids by opener

Holding around 20pts after, say, 1♡–1♠, bid game if you can. If that is unrealistic, jump in a second suit. If you have no second suit you may have to jump just the same.

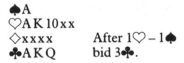 ♠A
♡AK10xx
◇xxxx      After 1♡–1♠
♣AKQ      bid 3♣.

### Jump bids by responder

Follow the same course:

(Opening 1♠):  with ♠AJxx
♡Jxxx
◇KQ
♣AKx   bid 3♣.

But do not jump in a major unless you hold a good suit.

(Opening 1♠):  with ♠AJxx
♡AK
◇KQx
♣Jxxx   bid 3◇.

3♡ is an appalling bid. Major suits are assumed to be serious.

† Perhaps you have noticed that in all three of these cases the jump was made in a three-card suit, when a longer one, albeit a poor one, was available. It is bad practice to introduce weak suits during strong bidding sequences.

### Responder

There are instances when you should not force at all, despite holding 16 or more points. This may be too tricky a subject at this stage, but we will give one example and leave it at that:

(Opening 1♡):   with ♠AQJx
♡x
♢AK109x
♣Axx

If you respond 3♢ and opener rebids 3NT, it is too late – without overbidding – to show your spade suit.

Looking ahead, like this, it is plain that a response of 2♢ will allow you to show your spades below game-level.

### Opener's rebids after a forcing bid

Bid naturally, we said in Part 1, and that is what you do. There is a dangerous heresy going about that you should make the same bid as you would have done over a simple response, but one higher. This leads to ludicrous results. For example, on the three hands below, after 1♡–1♠ you would bid 2♢ in each case.

But after 1♡–2♠ you should not mention the diamonds at all (remember: don't bid bad suits during strong sequences). Instead, clarify your hand to the best of your ability.

| a ♠Kx | b ♠Kx | c ♠Kx |
|---|---|---|
| ♡AJxxx | ♡AJxxx | ♡AQJ109 |
| ♢Qxxx | ♢Qxxx | ♢Qxxx |
| ♣Kx | ♣AQ | ♣xx |

On **a** rebid 2NT; on **b** 3NT, conveying the strength of the hand without being misleading about the quality of the hearts; and on **c** bid 3♡, stressing that the suit *has* quality.

Now look particularly at the second of these hands. You will remember our injunction not to jump the bidding during strong sequences; and here we are rebidding 3NT over 2♠.

But it is not a contradiction. If you have something useful to say you keep the bidding low, with, say, 3◇, 3♡ or 3♠; if you haven't you must distinguish between hand **a**, 2NT on 13pts, and hand **b**, 3NT or 16pts.

And this bid of 3NT does, in fact, say a lot: *i*) that your hearts are not strong enough to rebid, *ii*) that you have no sound second suit, *iii*) that you have no immediate support for partner's spades, and *iv*) that you have 16pts.

## Opposition action after an opening 4♡ or 4♠

Takeout doubles only operate against bids below game level: 3◇, 4◇, etc., so it is difficult to counter these blockbuster openings.

Bid a suit if it is strong enough, otherwise 4NT is for takeouts.

After pre-emptive openings of 5♣ or 5◇, the pace gets hotter still. A double is for penalties, but is also undertstood to be flexible. Partner can take out into a good major suit, and that can work well at times. At other times disaster is just around the corner!

In general the technique of bidding strong hands of all kinds is to keep the bidding as low as possible, allowing space for as many bids as possible before choosing the level of the final contract.

In the background there is always your trump suit, 4♡ or 4♠, or 3NT, to fall back into if you have had enough. Conversely, don't fall back into it if you want to go on, for you are in danger of your partner passing.

The need for bidding space is essential when you are looking for a slam by way of *cue bidding*, instead of Blackwood. *Andante*, now. Good players bypass Blackwood whenever they can, for it is unquestionably a blunt instrument crashing down with only one question and answer. Cue bidding is the delicate approach in which questions are asked and answered in turn to build up a complete picture of the two hands.

It can be likened to a leisurely conversation between two friends arranging to visit the theatre:

| | |
|---|---|
| 1♠ | 3♠ – Yes, we will. |
| 4♣ (*club* A) | 4◇ (*diamond* A) |

(agreeing the time and the pre-theatre rendezvous).

Now what seats can we afford? Back row of the circle (4♠) or the stalls (6♠ or 7♠)?

>4♠ – For my part
>the circle.
>
>>1 No bid – Agreed *or*
>>2 5♡ – Nonsense, I'm quite flush; together we ought to manage the stalls. (And I hold the heart ace.)
>
>1 5♠ – Still no *or*
>2 6♠ – Yes, all right.

Blackwood discovers how many aces there are, but not where they are. It is of no help on a hand like this:

♠KQxxx
♡AKJx
◇—
♣KQJx

After spades have been agreed as trumps, a slam is cold if partner holds either of the black aces. If you bid Blackwood and receive a reply of 5◇ you have no way of knowing which ace. So don't use Blackwood with a void.

When cue bidding, you first agree the trump suit, then bid your first-round controls – aces or voids – upwards, so that if one is omitted it is not there:

1♠ – 3♠
4♣ – 4♡ (control in hearts, but not in diamonds)

Later, if space allows and if you want to go on, you bid second-round controls, K x or a singleton.

With this hors d'oeuvre we shall stop. To go further into the complete meal would be beyond the scope of this book.

## Gerber

An ace-showing convention as Blackwood is, but the asking bid is 4♣ instead of 4NT and the replies begin at 4◇ (no ace). Some players use it instead of Blackwood; others in conjunction with it, confining Gerber to asking bids during no-trump bidding only. This is the better course.

However, everyone knows Blackwood, and it will do for you at present.

# 18 Doubling

**For takeout**

This is familiar to you now, and our view is that it is too little used in place of an overcall.

Two other points about the takeout double:

1 Partner of the responder may pass if holding nothing but strength in the opener's suit:

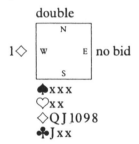

double

1◇   W   E   no bid

    ♠xxx
    ♡xx
    ◇QJ1098
    ♣Jxx

This can be passed so that the double is now for penalties. But to pass you must have powerful sequential trumps. With a woolly holding of Qxxx in opener's suit and 3-3-3 in the others you have to find a bid. Some players in these circumstances will respond 1NT; others will bid a three-card suit, say 1♠.

These are deep waters, but there is a good reason for avoiding a reply of 1NT, unless you are driven into a corner with no escape. After all, your partner asked you to bid a *suit* and will look upon a no-trump response as quite contrary.

2 A second double is also for takeout:

| | | | |
|---|---|---|---|
| 1◇ | double | 2◇ | no bid |
| no bid | double | no bid | ? |

The double was passed the first time because of the intervention. The second double makes a response mandatory.

**3** You can open the bidding *and* double for takeout.

1♡      1♠      no bid      no bid
double by opener is now for takeout

### For penalties

You know about these too. Be chary of doubling for penalties when your partner has not bid. Do so very firmly when your partner has:

2♣

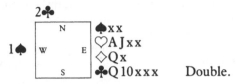

1♠   W   E   ♠xx ♡AJxx ◇Qx ♣Q10xxx     Double.

O joyous day! You are going to pick up a penalty of between 300 and 1700 – according to vulnerability, the fall of the cards, and not least, who the overcaller was!

Of course, you must use your judgement about such penalty doubles. The hand above will come as a nasty shock to the declarer, but this one is different:

2♣

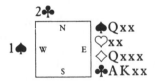

1♠   W   E   ♠Qxx ♡xx ◇Qxxx ♣AKxx

No shocks here. The declarer is expecting to lose the two top clubs, and your three spades to the queen (partner's suit) are a liability, not an asset. On this you bid 2NT.

Experience will guide you on when to double. It is a good basis for a decision to ask yourself: does my hand have a shock element?

### Doubles while competing

These were noted in the chapter on overcalling. You are saying, 'Partner, I believe they have overstepped the mark. Best not to go on, unless you have something unusual in the way of distribution.'

## Lead-directing doubles

These are usually, but not always, made against no-trump contracts and ask for a specific suit to be led.

| W | N | E | S |
|-----|--------|------|---------|
| 1♡ | no bid | 2♢ | no bid |
| 3NT | no bid | no bid | double |

This double means, 'Lead the suit bid on my right'; in this case diamonds. You should hold strong diamonds and have a fair chance of beating the contract provided a diamond is led.

If two suits are bid on your right, the double asks for the first to be led. To attract a lead of the second you need to double it on the way round.

*But* a lead-directing double after your side has bid overrides any other. Now it means, 'Lead our suit.'

You may say, 'But I always do,' but do you? Every player at some time is tempted on hands like this:

♠xx      after partner has bid spades and the opponents have
♡xx      ended up in 3NT.
♢Qxxx
♣QJ109x

You may reason: 'A spade lead is hopeless after such strong bidding. I'll have a go at the good-looking club suit.' Very occasionally it works. Much more often it doesn't; and when it doesn't your partner is justifiably aggrieved at not having had a spade lead.

To make certain of it, your partner – if strong enough in spades – should double 3NT, with the meaning, 'Forget what you're thinking about, lead my suit.'

It works the other way round, too.

| W | N | E | S |
|-----|--------|------|---------|
| 1♡ | 1♠ | 2♣ | no bid |
| 2NT | no bid | 3NT | double |

Without your double, your partner, whose spades are no great shakes, may try another suit. But suppose you have something like:

♠K10
♡xx
♢Axxx
♣Jxxxx

Plainly a spade is the best lead, and by doubling you say so. And note that this overrides the order, 'Bid the suit on my right'; in this case clubs, in favour of, 'Lead our suit.'

Lastly, in this section, a fun situation – although sometimes it is not so funny. If you and your partner have bid different suits and the opposition have ended in 3NT, you have a choice which even experts do not relish. No sound advice here, except possibly to choose your partner's suit in furtherance of good relations. If it turns out wrong, at least you have a good defence in the post-contract inquest!

## Lead-directing doubles against any contract

You may double any bid of the opposition *en passant* for a lead of that suit, specifically Blackwood responses and cue bids.

## Lightner doubles against slams

You don't double slams for penalties, remember, so such a double has a special meaning. It says, 'Find an unusual lead.' Doubler usually has a void and wants an immediate ruff.

Partner should have no difficulty then in leading a diamond from xx xxx xxxxxx Ax.

# 19  Pre-empts

It is amusing, although not very rewarding, to discuss hands with enormously long suits in them. There can be no exact answer to what to do with ten-card suits, except to say that **1** you may never get one; **2** you must keep a cool head and an iron nerve; and **3** you can go where your fancy takes you!

With this, for instance:

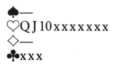

a somewhat wobbly case can be made for 1♡, 2♡, 3♡, 4♡ (not 5♡, which has a different meaning), 6♡ or 7♡. Or if it is late at night and you have a pliable partner, 2♣! Or, moving into the realms of fantasy, a psychic bid such as 1◇. At one time psychic bids were all the rage; no longer, thank goodness.

Enough of this. We will return to a more mundane pre-emptive level.

Weak-three openings depend on your position at the table.

In first or second position, stay with the advice in Part 1, but add one rider: do not open if your hand is suitable for a heart or spade contract.

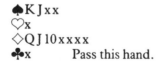

But in third position, after your partner has passed, you know there can be no game on your side. Your opening can therefore be stronger:

    ♠KJx
    ♡x
    ◇QJ10xxxx
    ♣Kx    Open 3◇ in third position.

You cannot open a pre-emptive weak three in fourth position; there is no one left to pre-empt. Occasionally you will – in a minor suit – for a different reason:

    ♠Ax
    ♡xx
    ◇xx
    ♣AQxxxxx

You can reasonably expect your bid to be passed round, allowing you to play in a part-score contract.

Because the purpose of pre-empts is to make life awkward for the other side, the higher the pre-empt the better. If you can open 4◇ or 5◇ instead of 3◇, do so.

This is a reasonable hand for a pre-emptive 5◇:

    ♠x
    ♡—
    ◇KJ10xxxxx
    ♣K10xx

And great fun. Your opponents, if they hold all the cards, have to discover whether hearts or spades is their suit and at what level to play: game, small slam or grand slam, and all beginning at the five-level.

### Other pre-empts

As an overcall, jump three levels:

1♠

with ♠x
♡Kx
◇xx
♣KQxxxxxx   bid 4♣.

> Responder can pre-empt over partner's
> opening bid – but infrequently, holding, say,
> an eight-card suit with no tops in it:
>
> (Opening 1◇):   with ♠—
> ♡QJxxxxx
> ◇xx
> ♣Qxx   bid 3♡.
>
> Because pre-empts vulnerable are stronger (or
> ought to be stronger) than non-vulnerable,
> responder can raise on slightly less, say 14pts.
>
> In Part 1, you were told that responder, hold-
> ing 16pts or more, should usually jump to
> *game* in opener's suit. It follows that 3◇–4◇
> carries a different message.
>
> (Opening 3◇):   with ♠x
> ♡xxx
> ◇Q10xx
> ♣Kxxxx
>
> You want to put more pressure still on your
> left-hand opponent. Bid 4◇ to increase the
> pre-empt.
>
> With a strong suit facing a weak three, plenty
> of points and some distribution, bid game in
> your suit:
>
> (Opening 3◇):   with ♠AKQ10xxx
> ♡x
> ◇xx
> ♣AKJ   bid 4♠.

Without such a good holding, try for game in
your suit:

with ♠AQ10xxx
♡AKxx
◇Qx
♣x                    bid 3♠.

This is forcing. Your partner can revert to 4◇
or bid 4♠ with some spade support; say Kx.

But note that both these spade bids are on
strong suits, either self-contained or requiring
minimal support.

To respond 3♠ on AKxxx is to go down
among the dead men.

With a void facing a weak three and no strong
suit, pass; but raise partner's suit to game with
19pts plus.

# 20   Declarer

In no field of activity has skill or genius emerged without a base of discipline. No tennis player won Wimbledon without the discipline of hard practice. Newton could not have propounded his theory of dynamics without the discipline of constant observation. A Beethoven is first disciplined on the hard graft of the scales.

A declarer's first discipline is to look at two hands clearly and as a whole. From that emerges a plan. It may be a solid plan based on lines of play suggested in Part 1. It may be a plan based on certain assumptions. It may be one, necessary because the hand has been overbid, which depends on the wildest improbabilities. Even that is better than none.

Of course plans can go wrong. If they do, that means adopting plan B, not giving up the ghost. And at the back of your mind is not exactly a plan, but a hope that the defenders will make mistakes. A hope which, in inexperienced company, you can safely call an assumption.

And if they haven't yet made a mistake in the hand you are playing now, help them along. Tempt mistakes. Lead an extra trump and watch while someone throws away the suit you hoped they would throw away. Count nothing lost until the thirteenth trick has been gathered.

And what about the first and second tricks? Even quite good players can err by taking them too quickly and then making their plan. It may be too late:

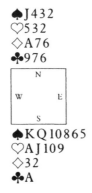

♠J432
♡532
◇A76
♣976

♠KQ10865
♡AJ109
◇32
♣A

You are in 4♠ and the *diamond* king is led, which you take with the ace. What sort of a hand is it? You have no ruffs in dummy, no side suit to set up. Your contract will win only if you can hold your heart losers to one.

The odds are heavily in favour of the heart honours being divided, so your chances are good – provided you take two finesses. You have one entry with the *spade* jack after the ace has been taken out, and no other.

No other? You are there already at the first trick. You must finesse the heart immediately to make your contract.

That was a play at trick 2. We could show you (but we won't because it is beyond the scope of this book) plenty of hands in which if you play an ace at trick 1 – even an ace facing a singleton – you will go down. Such is the importance of the first trick.

## The art of losing the lead

By now you are well versed in establishing a suit by first losing a trick in it, but there are other reasons for losing the lead. In general it will be because your hand contains awkward holdings, tenaces such as K J x, and you would prefer the defenders to play the next card. Then, if you can, you safely get off lead by deliberately losing a trick.

You will also frequently be trying to lose the lead to the *safe hand*, with such a combination as this:

```
        K 9 x
Jxx  ┌──────┐  A Q 10 x
     │      │
     └──────┘
       xxx (you)
```

Leading from your hand, you put up the 9 in dummy. East now takes two tricks, but has to give you the third.

Of course, if West had woken up and played the jack you would have lost all three, but the inexperienced West has given up the hand and is thinking more along the lines of a gin and tonic.

The next examples of losing the lead should open up new horizons in your play of the cards:

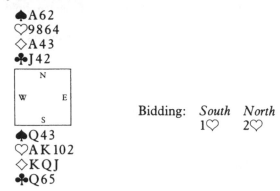

♠A62
♡9864
◇A43
♣J42

Bidding:    *South   North*
　　　　　　1♡　　2♡

♠Q43
♡AK102
◇KQJ
♣Q65

(In parenthesis, although this chapter is about play, how many of you playing South will have been tempted to bid again? Seventeen points, yes, but a very bad seventeen, because: **1** the hand has no shape; **2** the points have serious defects and won't all be working for you: KQJ isn't worth 6pts, your jack will probably fall under an ace and be worth nothing, and the Qxx in clubs is far from gilt-edged. But when and when not to count points belongs to another book.)

Anyway, when dummy goes down you are glad you stopped in 2♡, and even that presents a problem. We will look at how the hand might be played.

After an opening diamond lead, you draw trumps, lose the third round and win the diamond return. Next you play the *spade* ace, then low to the queen, which loses, and is followed by another spade trick by the defence. You again win the diamond return and play clubs. The queen loses to the king, the jack to the ace, and a third club is lost. One down.

Now think about the hand from the beginning. Your possible losers are a trump, two spades and three clubs. How can you avoid one of them? By losing the lead at the right moment, and forcing the defence to lead spades or clubs. Once *they* lead either suit, you are home.

Now follow this train of thought further. In order to force the defence to lead a spade or a club, you need to make sure they cannot lead a diamond . . . otherwise *they* will get off lead in that suit and put you back to where you started. So you play three rounds of diamonds, leaving none in either hand; if they now play a diamond when they get in, you simply ruff in one hand and discard a losing spade or club in the other, making your contract that way.

So the picture is complete: **1** take the opening diamond lead; **2** draw two rounds of trumps with the A K; **3** cash two more rounds of diamonds; **4** put the opposition in by leading the third round of trumps and losing to the queen. Your remaining cards are:

♠A62
♡9
◇—
♣Q42

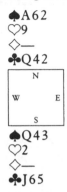

♠Q43
♡2
◇—
♣J65

Any lead by the defence gives you your contract. If they lead a spade, try the queen; if the king is put on top of it, take the ace and lead a spade back. After one more trick the defence will be forced to lead clubs, and you make a club trick.

With this kind of play we are back with the declarer's question, 'What if. . .?' but in a different sense. In Part 1 it was asked negatively: 'What if . . . one hand has Jxxx; can I avoid losing a trick?' Now it is positive. 'What if . . . I can force a defender to lead a certain suit? Yes, that will give me my contract.'

For example, now that you know all about finessing you can approach a finesse from an opposite view. 'Yes, it is a 50-50 chance, but what if . . . I can make a defender lead the suit?'

A J x      K 10 x

If a defender leads the suit there is no finesse left. Three tricks are a certainty.

♠QJxxx
♡Kxx
♢Ax
♣Kxx

♠AKxxxx
♡Ax
♢Jx
♣AJx

You are in 6♠, and West leads the *diamond* king. Your possible losers are a diamond and a club, if the finesse is wrong. But you need not finesse.

Take the *diamond* ace, draw trumps, play *heart* A K and ruff a heart, then lead the *diamond* jack. From the lead, the *diamond* queen is known to be with West, so now your position is:

♠Jxx
♡—
♢—
♣Kxx

♠Axx
♡—
♢—
♣AJx

West can only lead a club into your A J x, or give a ruff and discard.

That was not too difficult because the lead pinpointed the *diamond* queen. You can throw the lead into a particular hand by other means, by a loser-on-loser play as described in Part 1 or often by tricking a sleepy defence.

Suppose the diamonds in the above hand had been:

Ax

xx

You would have made the same play, but leading the second diamond from dummy. If East puts up a high card and wins the trick, a club will come next through your A J and the finesse is your only hope. But this time it is East who is asleep and plays low. West has to take the trick and you win just the same.

We told you before: more contracts are made because of poor defence than by any other means!

The plays described in the last two hands are known as *elimination plays* because you eliminate one or two suits from the hand, leaving the defence no option but to lead the one you wish. They can go on to be quite advanced, but this is the basis of them.

It is not our intention to take you too far, into end plays, trump coups, squeezes and such manoeuvres; they can wait for *The Second Bridge Book*! However, as a foretaste, only to be lightly touched on, here are two interesting forms of play.

**1 Avoidance.**

♠AKxxx
♡xx
◇KQx
♣Jxx

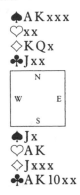

♠Jx
♡AK
◇Jxxx
♣AK10xx

You are in 3NT after East has bid hearts, and a heart is led. If the club finesse fails, hearts will be cleared and you are held to eight tricks. Alternatively, you can play on diamonds and hope for a 3-3 break, but this is against the odds.

In fact you are back on familiar territory, aiming to take your ninth trick at trick 2, but with a difference. East's bid of hearts surely places the *diamond* ace in that hand. At trick 2, cross to dummy with a spade and lead a low diamond away from the K Q; if East rises with the ace, you have your contract with three diamonds, two clubs, two spades and two hearts; if East plays low, switch to clubs and give up a trick – the contract is made with four clubs, two hearts, two spades and a diamond.

2  Dummy reversal.

Many players who regard a crossruff as a simple exercise look on the reverse dummy as some arcane mystery. But if you count your trumps correctly in a suit contract it presents no special problem.

The difficulty most players have with a reverse dummy is recognizing when it should be played. The signal is when you have a singleton in your own hand.

When dummy has a singleton, you automatically ruff losers there and draw trumps later from your own hand. In dummy reversals you ruff in your own hand and draw trumps from dummy. Here is an example:

♠AKJ
♡Axxxx
♢AQJ
♣xx

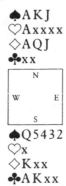

♠Q5432
♡x
♢Kxx
♣AKxx

You are in 7♠ and the *heart* king is led. You can see eleven tricks. Ruffing two clubs in dummy would provide the last two, but your trumps are so paltry that if you use the king and jack for ruffs you must lose a trump trick.

Playing a dummy reversal you ruff three hearts in your own hand; the third with the queen – making altogether six trump tricks, three diamonds, two clubs and two hearts, the fifth one having been established.

You can be defeated only by a 4-1 break in trumps or an unlucky heart distribution. However, this is the *only* way you can make the grand slam.

Rather than pursue such plays into tiger country, we shall now take you back to the art of losing the lead, and perhaps to your surprise, a simple contract of 1NT, passed all round.

But, and here is where you read carefully, this is tiger country too. Many a player who has studiously learned about end plays and reverse dummys is flummoxed in a part-score hand. Indeed, a 1NT contract, with the points divided roughly 20-20 between declarer and defence, can be a demon hand to make and to defend, and one in which skill will really show.

Here is a typical example:

♠1042
♡K973
◇952
♣A64

♠AJ3
♡J42
◇KJ8
♣K873

Contract 1NT. The *club* queen is led, immediately depressing your hopes of making three club tricks.

And what else? If you play this hand at all aggressively you may be †† held to four tricks, three down. So your intention is deliberately to lose the lead, as often and as safely as you can, so as to get the lead back to you from the defenders. In that way your tenaces may produce two tricks, and possibly the *heart* 9 and the *diamond* 8 or 9 may pull their weight.

It isn't going to be easy, because any sensible defender, also with a hand full of awkward holdings like yours, will be doing exactly the same thing – playing passively and not giving tricks away. So it becomes a battle of attrition, and one of the more fascinating examples of bridge trench-warfare. Whoever loses the lead most effectively may come to the seventh trick: 1NT made, or one down.

It is not possible to trace how this hand might go, but you begin playing as you intend to go on. Hoping that the club lead was not from a five-card suit, you take the first two clubs, then lead a club back. The defence, after taking two clubs, has to lead to you. And so on.

There is as much delight in playing and making a humble contract like this as there is in bringing off an exotic slam. And perhaps you can understand that the expert who put forward the proposition that his partner could play all the slams if he were allowed to play the part scores was more cunning than philanthropic.

The last was an extreme, but not uncommon, example. In many part-score contracts you will be doing the same thing: losing the lead in the hope of getting a favourable lead back.

Here is another example of a difficult part score to play:

♠A x
♡Q x x
◇J x x x
♣Q J x x

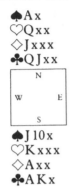

♠J 10 x
♡K x x x
◇A x x
♣A K x

You opened 1♡, West overcalled 1♠ and your partner bid 2♡, passed all round. Whether you think your partner's bid should have been 1NT is neither here nor there. You are playing in 2♡ with a straggly seven-card trump suit. The *spade* king is led, on which East plays the 9, obviously showing a doubleton at best.

We know exactly how beginners, and many average players, will view this hand. They will look on the trumps as being too pathetic to be touched, fearing that, if they are played, control of the hand will be lost.

Yet trumps must be played. Take the first trick in dummy, cross to your *club* ace and lead a heart towards the queen. Because West bid, the queen will probably win. Lead a trump back, ducking in your hand. Only very unlucky distribution can now prevent your taking eight tricks.

††    The lesson is – and it is true most of the time – the worse your trumps, the more necessary it is to play them.

## Safety plays

You were shown one in Part 1, where you held A Q 9 x x facing K 10 x x, and your play was the high honour (in this case the ace) from the hand with two, so as to ensure a finesse against the J x x x in either direction.

Now take the 10 away, leaving A Q 9 x x facing K x x, and one finesse position has disappeared. If J 10 x x is over A Q 9 x x, you can do nothing about it. Play the king first, and you have ensured that one option remains.

Next consider A 10 x x x facing K 9 x x. If you cannot afford to lose any tricks at all you must play out A K and hope the drop is 2-2. More often you can afford to lose one trick in the suit, but not two: so to guard against Q J x x in one hand, you play low from either hand and cover whatever your opponent plays.

There are dozens of recognized safety plays in bridge, some quite complicated. No more about them here.

Our last comment is on *counting*. It is not too difficult to count *points* in the defenders' hands. If one of them has bid, you will naturally place most of the high cards in that hand. If a player who has not bid turns up with two aces and a king, you will assume a missing queen to be in the other hand, otherwise you would have expected an opening bid with 13pts.

Distribution is another matter. Of course you count the trump suit, any side suit you are interested in and the length of the enemy's suit in no trumps. You should also be able to remember how many cards have been played in all four suits.

But the count, say half-way through the hand, of how many cards each defender has left in each suit is beyond the range of most average players. When you can do it, a whole new world of cardplay opens up, but it involves a particular kind of thinking which can be extraordinarily difficult. (The authors themselves disagree on this point, which shows the difference in playing standards between them. J.F. knows how easy bridge is; and J.G. how difficult it can be!)

Some hands can be counted easily. South opens 3♡ and you play in 6♠. The only trouble with the contract is that same combination in clubs:

AJx ⬜ K10x

You need to pick up the queen for twelve tricks.

South has seven hearts, follows three times to trumps and three times to diamonds – distribution 7-3-3-0. North must have the *club* queen. (Just in case South opened with a six-card suit and has a singleton club, you play the ace first and then finesse. Either way the contract is cold.)

As you play more and gain experience you will find yourself counting more. At this stage don't try too hard. At least don't try to count all the distribution in all the hands. You will find it painfully slow, or rather your opponents will, and that will take the sparkle out of the game. It *is* meant to be fun, remember!

# 21 Defence

Introspection is an analysis of oneself, which as often as not leads to self-pity. This is the attitude adopted by nearly all beginners when they are defending on poor cards. They commiserate with themselves, more or less give up, play the cards carelessly and so help declarer to make a contract.

Awareness, on the other hand – although it includes awareness of oneself – also takes in everything that is going on around. An aware defender looks positively at a poor hand, assumes that partner has some values, regards the merits and demerits of dummy, and sets about trying to defeat the contract.

Very little in bridge is negative. If you think negatively you get negative results:

♠109x    You are on lead against 3NT. Alackaday!
♡xxxx   What a frightfully depressing lot. We've no
◇xx      chance this time, to be sure.
♣Jxxx

Now think positively. If the other side has reached 3NT with 26pts your partner has 13. Big guns, those 13pts, but your hand matters too. You have several positive things to do.

1   Forget about your four-card suits. Try to lead into your partner's hand. The *spade* 10 must be the obvious choice.

2   Hold on to those four clubs to the jack; you never know. (You didn't lead clubs because if you are ever going to take a trick in this hand it will be with that jack.)

3   Don't show by word, gesture, look or sigh that you are holding a bundle of rubbish. If you are going to behave other than neutrally (which you shouldn't) don't look hangdog but play with an air of ease and confidence.

The defence has one standing advantage over the declarer. Theirs is the opening lead, and at this moment the tempo is on their side. Tempo is a precious asset, too easily given away.

An easy example is the defence to a small slam, when you are leading from:

♠xx   (trumps)
♡Axx
◇Qxxx
♣xxxx

The lead of the ace will probably (subject to the bidding) return the tempo to the declarer; a low diamond from your queen, looking for the king in your partner's hand will, if successful, leave the tempo with you.

Do you ask why your partner shouldn't have the *heart* king? The answer is that declarer is much less likely to have bid a slam with A K missing in one suit than with an ace and a king missing in different suits.

The following hand illustrates exactly how the opening lead can gain the tempo – or give it away.

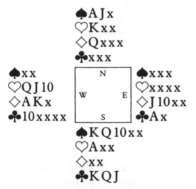

```
            ♠AJx
            ♡Kxx
            ◇Qxxx
            ♣xxx
♠xx                      ♠xxx
♡QJ10       N            ♡xxxx
◇AKx     W     E         ◇J10xx
♣10xxxx                  ♣Ax
            S
            ♠KQ10xx
            ♡Axx
            ◇xx
            ♣KQJ
```

South is in 4♠. A lead of the *heart* queen sets the tempo and defeats the contract. Had you chosen the *diamond* ace and switched to the *heart* queen, declarer draws trumps, plays a low diamond towards the queen, and later discards a heart. The tempo would have been lost to the other side.

Alas! the opening lead is not often as simple as this. In aiming to keep the tempo, you often give it away. How often does a hand end with the comment, 'If a spade (or whatever) had been led it would have gone down'?

One or two further points about leading against no-trump contracts:

- From A K x x, lead the ace and look around; with five, of course, lead the fourth highest.
- With a choice of suits like these:

> A Q 10 x
> 10 x x x

choose the second; the first, although more aggressive, almost certainly gives a trick away. However, with five of either, lead your fourth highest.

And two generalities:

1 If in doubt, do not automatically reach for the unbid suit. Take the bidding into account, and think. The unbid suit too often turns out to be the one in which declarer is strongest. Bidding like this is quite common:

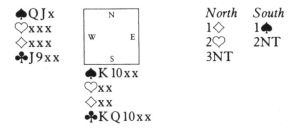

|  | ♠Q J x | | North | South |
|---|---|---|---|---|
|  | ♡x x x | | 1◇ | 1♠ |
|  | ◇x x x | | 2♡ | 2NT |
|  | ♣J 9 x x | | 3NT | |
|  | ♠K 10 x x | | | |
|  | ♡x x | | | |
|  | ◇x x | | | |
|  | ♣K Q 10 x x | | | |

So much for a club lead from West!

2 However, if spades are not bid there is at least an inference that a spade should be led. Put it no higher than that. The accepted thinking is that everyone bids spades who can, and if they haven't, on the way to a NT contract, they are weak in the suit. Further thinking should make it clear that this is arrant nonsense. Declarer and dummy can have A K Q J between them, and yet neither hold a four-card suit. Nonetheless, the inference is there, and at least worth consideration.

## Leading against suit contracts

Only one further point. You have no difficulty in leading a singleton, hoping for a ruff. But not enough players consider the possibility of a singleton in their partner's hand. Of course not. That means stretching the imagination beyond their own cards! Yet it makes sense, and the lead of a five- or six-card suit can pay dividends.

# MUD leads

There always has been, and always will be, a difficulty for partner in distinguishing between doubleton leads, 8 6; and top of nothing, 8 6 4. MUD stands for middle, up, down; from three cards MUD players lead the cards in the order of **6 8 4**. It has advantages and disadvantages, and this note is for the record. We suggest you keep to the orthodox lead of top of nothing.

With four small cards, say 8 6 4 2, lead the third and then go upwards. The lead of your lowest shows an honour.

# After taking a trick

Sometimes the opening lead strikes gold; more often it doesn't. When it doesn't, a great weight descends on *the defender who first obtains the lead*. This is often the crucial moment in the defence.

Here are some of your considerations:

● Partner's opening lead: should it be returned?
● What *did* the opening lead mean?

```
              KQJ3
   6 (led)  ┌─────┐  A985
            │     │
            └─────┘
```

The 6 was a singleton or a doubleton. Are you going to take dummy's queen with your ace and return the suit for a ruff? Or do you assume a doubleton, duck, get in with your ace of trumps and play back A x for a ruff? (The answer to this is that doubletons are much more common than singletons and, no other factors being present, you should duck. If you are wrong you will get a dark look from your partner. Say 'Sorry,' and try to change the subject.)

● Dummy has a good suit to be established and an ace outside. Should you aim straight to knock out the entry, if necessary leading K x x? Is that a priority over returning partner's suit? (The answer is usually yes.)

● About how many points does your partner hold? What will be the declarer's likely line of play? Are you to lead aggressively or passively?

You formulate some sort of a plan. Not such an exact one as declarer because of the obvious disadvantage that you cannot know what your partner holds, but a plan just the same – one elastic enough to be altered according to the way the play goes.

If you do this you will be ahead of all run-of-the-mill defenders. Most declarers make a plan of some kind. Most defenders don't. They follow meekly to declarer's leads and, if they get in, make orthodox returns.

This is the sort of thing:

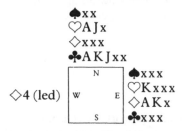

♠xx
♡AJx
◇xxx
♣AKJxx

◇4 (led)

♠xxx
♡Kxxx
◇AKx
♣xxx

The contract is 4♠ by South and your partner leads the *diamond* 4. You take the trick with the king.

You can easily discover whether you have three diamond tricks in defence. Lead the *diamond* ace next. Your partner follows with the 2. As the lead of the 4 was the fourth highest, the 2 shows a five-card suit. Declarer began with only two diamonds.

You are not enamoured of the hand. If there is a finesse in clubs it will be right, and the clubs will also provide discards. No point whatever in passively playing another diamond.

So what next? You must assume your partner has a trick in trumps, say Qxx; and, if your side is to have any chance of winning a fourth trick before clubs are played, the *heart* queen.

You lead a heart. Your assumptions are correct and the contract goes one down, declarer losing two diamonds, a heart and a trump.

Had your assumptions been wrong it wouldn't have mattered. The contract was going to make anyway. You gave yourself the best chance.

The difficulty with this hand, as our more critical readers will observe, is reconciling the aggressive lead of a heart with our frequent advice to be passive. It is the perennial question which troubles even the most expert players. The best way to find an answer is to ask yourself the question: is the declarer, if I play passively, likely to succeed? If the answer is 'yes', you must attack.

At bridge you must not only think, but you must think about the right things. We know that almost everyone thinks, or we suppose they do, because they take so long to play a card. But what they are actually thinking *about* is a mystery. It is probably, but not always, something to do with bridge ('We should have made that slam.'/'What a stupid partner I've got.'/'I'd love a Scotch and water.') and, if it is connected with the hand being played, almost certainly a negative thought ('Nothing to be done here; I might as well lead a diamond.'). Which is where we began.

If the answer to the question: can declarer succeed if I play passively? is 'no', we ask you to look back to the 1NT hand in the last chapter. On that hand any aggression by you at any moment, even the tiniest little forward move, smooths the path of the declarer. You need to be so passive as to make an iron mountain look like a ball of fire.

And incidentally, the play of that 1NT hand, with both sides straining not to take tricks, will be as entertaining as any in bridge.

### Suit-length signals

When the declarer leads, the correct play is to follow suit upwards with an odd number of cards, downwards with an even number. This is critically important in cases like this:

K Q J 10 x (no entries)

873     A 64    South is playing in no trumps.

Your partner is going to hold up the ace to cut declarer off from dummy. You play the 3 followed by the 7. Your partner can count you for three cards, and the declarer for two, and puts the ace up on the second round.

Had you held 7 3 only you play the 7 followed by the 3, and partner will hold up the ace until the third round. Discipline yourself to play the small cards in the right order.

You will not make suit-length signals on your *partner's* leads in no trumps. They become too confusing. For example, if you begin a peter with an 8 – from 8 2 – it will probably be read as encouragement, asking for the suit to be continued. An exception, however, is when you hold four cards in the suit your partner leads; then you should peter to show length (and indeed encouragement).

That is in no trumps. Don't mix it up with suit contracts when, of course, you will continue to play high–low to show a doubleton.

When returning a suit to your partner you can show your length, against any contract. You hold A 9 3 and take your partner's lead with the ace; return the 9 to show you began with three. With four cards such as A932 return the 2.

But be realistic. With A1095, return the 10. It is a greater priority to run through declarer's honour on your left than to give the count.

## Second player plays low

There are many exceptions to this generality. We noted some in Part 1; without carrying the subject too far, here are two others:

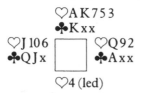

♥AK753<br>♣Kxx
♥J106    ♥Q92<br>♣QJx    ♣Axx
♥4 (led)

Declarer is beginning to set up the heart suit and intends to duck in both hands, hoping to put East in and avoid a damaging club lead from you in the West seat. You must go in with your 10 the first time, and the jack if the suit is played again. Declarer cannot now duck the suit without letting you in to lead clubs.

This kind of play occurs frequently:

♠xx (trumps)<br>◇xxx
◇J53<br>♣xx

Declarer, having eliminated the other suits, has nothing but trumps and diamonds left in the two hands, and leads a diamond from dummy. A dozy West will play low; an alert one goes in with the jack.

Here are the cards in all four hands:

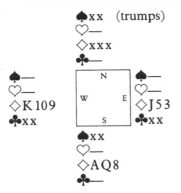

If East plays low, declarer covers with the 8 and West, after taking the 9, can only lead a diamond back from K 10 into A Q, or a club which gives a ruff and discard.

It is, admittedly, dreadfully easy to go to sleep on East's cards. But that is what bridge is all about, thinking.

You might get by if you thought as far as, 'This high card is no use to me; I might as well play it.' It will certainly score in the next example, but it is better that you know *why* you are playing a high card.

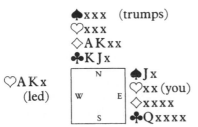

Your partner leads the *heart* A K and another, and you are about to ruff. Dozy East will ruff low; a half-awake East might think, 'The jack of trumps is no use to me; I'll put it up.' A good player will certainly ruff with the jack, for positive reasons. It has a good chance of promoting a trump trick in partner's hand.

Here is the trump suit in full:

```
        x x x
10 x x  ┌───┐  J x
        │   │
        └───┘
       A K Q x x
```

The jack is overruffed by the queen, and now partner makes a trump trick.

This is familiarly known as an uppercut. You can even uppercut, if the cards lie favourably, by ruffing with a 7 instead of a 2.

That was all about ruffing. Next is not ruffing:

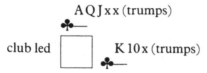

```
           A Q J x x (trumps)
           ♣—
club led  ┌───┐  K 10 x (trumps)
          │   │
          └───┘
                 ♣—
```

Declarer ruffs the club lead high with the jack. If you overruff with the king that is the only trump trick you will take. Discard instead from another suit, and now the trumps look like this:

```
      A Q x x
     ┌───┐  K 10 x
     │   │
     └───┘
```

You make two.

†     Not ruffing is generally to be preferred in defence if you have a good trump holding: J 10 x x, K Q x, Q 10 x x. With trumps like these you should have avoided a singleton or doubleton lead in the first place. You don't want to ruff, you want to harass the declarer in the trump suit. J 10 x x is often a harassment; after a ruff, J 10 x is of no consequence.

## Discarding

The bidding and the sight of dummy may help you in your choice of discards. Quite often they won't, and even experts find this a difficult problem.

Here is a general rule which, like any generality, should be amended when there is a better clue: prefer to discard from a five- or a three-card suit than from a four-card one.

The other imperative about this difficult subject is to keep going smoothly. As declarer runs off a long trump suit and you feel like squirming, conceal your discomfort. It is not cheating for a declarer to gather information from the behaviour of the defenders, so don't give any. Anticipate the moment when you have to make a painful discard and, when it comes, be ready. If you bare a king after a long agonizing pause you may gain marks for technical merit, but that will be your only reward.

### False carding

A huge subject, and one to be handled with the utmost care. Defenders who false card pointlessly and continually are quite infuriating, and baffle their partners far more than they do the declarer. However, there are occasions when a false card is obligatory:

```
          A J 2
(you) Q 10 4 ┌─────┐ 6 5 3
          └─────┘
          K 9 8 7
```

Declarer finesses the jack and then plays the ace. You can see now that the whole suit is against you, so you must drop the queen under the ace. There is a good chance now that declarer will come back with a finesse of the 9 to your 10.

There is, finally, one occasion in defence when you would like to signal a ruff-to-be but cannot. That is when your partner leads an ace (from A K) and you hold Qx. You may play high–low with any two cards up to Jx, but the play of a queen under the ace is reserved for another meaning. It says, 'I have QJ, and you can safely underlead your king at trick 2 if you wish to put me in.'

At bridge (whatever your opinion) the cards roughly even out in the long run. The winners are those who make the most of poor hands, and effectively that means saving tricks in defence.

But perhaps you don't mind if you win or lose so long as you enjoy yourself. You probably think that bidding, and playing and making a contract, are the most enjoyable parts of bridge.

If so, you are missing a lot. Nothing, in our opinion, is so satisfying as beating a contract which at first sight appeared unbeatable.

# 22  Duplicate bridge

This book has been about rubber bridge, the game played among friends and families and at some bridge clubs. Duplicate bridge is the form used for competitions.

In duplicate the hands come to you slotted into boards. After being played they are returned to the board and passed on for another pair to play, and so on. You compete not so much against your opponents as against all the other pairs who are playing the same hands as you are.

And because everybody plays the same hands, the luck of picking up good or bad cards is eliminated.

Each hand is a separate entity. The board tells the state of vulnerability and the dealer. Score for making a game is 300 non-vulnerable and 500 vulnerable; a part score is worth 50. Honours are not counted.

There are two kinds of play: teams of four, as shown on the BBC TV programme *Grand Slam*, in which caution plays a part; and pairs, when you and your partner are taking on all comers, without regard to the rest of a team. In pairs the sky can be the limit.

Apart from the scoring on individual boards, there are various methods of overall scoring. They are not important at this time, but whatever the method they all add broadly to an end result that the better you do on a hand, the higher your score.

The principal way in which pairs differs from rubber bridge (other than luck) is that in rubber bridge you are often content to take a game; in pairs you need overtricks, all the tricks you can make. Even one overtrick scored by a partnership, when no other did, will come to a top score all on its own. One extra trick made by a pair in defence adds up to the same result, so unlike rubber bridge, the scoring difference between one down and two down, or 4♠ or 5♠ made, can be very wide.

The other factor is vulnerability. A vulnerable game scores 500, plus, say, 100 for 3NT, totalling 600. Opponents can go two down doubled vulnerable or three down doubled non-vulnerable (500 in each case) and achieve a winning result.

Duplicate is much slower than rubber bridge, as every pair struggles for a maximum score. There are also certain procedures, such as using the word 'stop' before making any jump or pre-emptive bid – for example an opening 3◇ is 'Stop. 3◇.' (You should also do this at rubber bridge, the purpose being to allow time for the next bidder to stop and think, differentiating that pause from an unethical long pause and then a pass.) There are other procedural differences too, but you will find out about these when you enter the world of competition.

For those who wish to test their skill or have aspirations in the game, duplicate it has to be. It will either provide you reassurance about your ability or bring you down to earth with a jolt.

For your next stage in bridge, 'Understanding Duplicate' by John Gullick describes the precise differences between rubber and duplicate. It doubles as an entertainment, centred on a mythical bridge club and its players, how they think and the mistakes they make.

Direct from Wimbledon Bridge Enterprises, 6 Walnut Tree Cottages, London SW19 5DN or from leading booksellers.

'Witty and, unlike most bridge books, lives up to its title.' – Bob Rowlands.

# 23 What bridge is all about

One thing bridge is not about is mathematics. Arithmetic will carry you some way, but not far. Much more than that it is detective work, making deductions from the facts and reasonable assumptions from what is going on around you.

The weatherman does this. If he were a run-of-the-mill bridge player he would state today's temperature and add that he had no idea of what was going to happen next – whether to draw trumps, ruff, stand on his head or announce a heatwave. He doesn't. He draws inferences from the information he receives from satellites, computers and weather ships, and makes a forecast. So also do amateur forecasters who throw a straw into the wind or feel their rheumatism coming on; they infer that rain is on the way.

In bridge, far too many players scan a hand briefly, register little or nothing, then play for impossibilities – or possibilities so rare that they are equivalent to a weatherman announcing after a flurry of snow that a new ice-age was on the way.

You are beyond that stage. Now perhaps you listen to the bidding, look at the cards and from what you see and hear make a plan. It is probably only half a plan, based on conjecture. Now we want you to take the first steps into the world of inference and assumption. With such weapons you will benefit in the same way that the first tennis player who served overhead left behind all the underhand players.

It is a broad subject, really belonging to a later book. At this time we shall give examples to start you off on the detective trail. You will see that some deductions you can make are positive; others, like the reason why the dog didn't bark at night, are negative. Here we go.

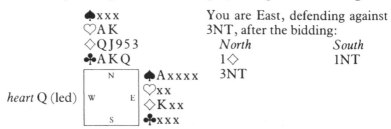

♠xxx
♡AK
◇QJ953
♣AKQ

*heart* Q (led)

♠Axxxx
♡xx
◇Kxx
♣xxx

You are East, defending against 3NT, after the bidding:

| North | South |
| --- | --- |
| 1◇ | 1NT |
| 3NT | |

Dummy takes the heart and leads the *diamond 3*.

First your assessment of the hand, beginning with partner's points. Yes, partner could have just enough points to hold *heart* QJ and one high card outside, the *diamond* ace or the *spade* king.

Now can you draw any inference from declarer's lead of *diamond 3*?

You think: 'Surely declarer should have led dummy's queen and captured my king with the ace. Why not? Presumably because declarer doesn't hold the ace. In that case I shall make my king next time round.

'Whoa a minute. If declarer hasn't the *diamond* ace, my partner has, and it may be the only entry to the heart suit. I must put up the king now, clear the hearts and leave partner with the ace as an entry to the established hearts.

'Could this inference be wrong? It might. Declarer might be foregoing the diamond finesse, simply playing up to the ace and back again. It seems unlikely, because dummy has plenty of entries.

'And here's the clincher. If declarer holds the *diamond* ace it doesn't matter what I do. The contract is on ice with four diamonds, two hearts and three clubs.'

So you rise with *diamond* king, return a heart, and 3NT is defeated.

Next a negative inference by declarer:

♠QJxx
♡Qx
◇KJ9x
♣xxx

♠AKxxx
♡Jx
◇A10xx
♣xx

The bidding went (both sides vulnerable):

| South | West | North | East |
|-------|------|-------|------|
| 1♠ | 2♣ | 2♠ | 3♣ |
| — | — | 3♠ | all pass |

West leads the *spade* 4. The losers are two clubs, two hearts, and a diamond if the finesse fails. Possibly one down.

Why the trump lead? Inference: West's clubs are broken, probably headed by AQ. Why not the ace from *heart* AK? Inference: West doesn't hold the *heart* K. That means that East probably has two kings.

What about the distribution? West certainly hasn't five hearts (otherwise 2♡ would have been the overcall), and may have only three. Should the play reveal that East has three trumps and three clubs, that hand will contain at least five hearts, perhaps six, and a shortage in diamonds. Furthermore, this was a pretty light vulnerable overcall by West, holding clubs headed by AQ(J) and only one ace outside. Assumption: West is likely to hold the missing *diamond* queen.

Conclusion: finesse the *diamond* jack, and make the contract.

Now a deduction from the bidding. Both sides are vulnerable:

| West | North | East | South |
|------|-------|------|-------|
| 1♠ | 2♣ | 4♠ | ? |

♠xxxx
♡x
◇Axxx
♣xxxx

No deduction : 'It's all over.' Pass.

Positive deduction: 'My partner wouldn't have overcalled vulnerable without a good suit and something outside; and also, because I have four spades, a void (or, at worst, a singleton) spade. If the "something outside" is in diamonds we might even make 5♣; if it is in hearts we should get away with two down. And there's always a chance we shall push them too high into 5♠.' Bid 5♣.

And again:

♠x
♡A K J 10 x
♢A Q x x x
♣K x

You open 1♡, and the bidding, with the opposition silent, goes:

1♡ – 1♠
2♢ – 2♠
3♢ – 3♠

Negative or wrong deduction: 'My partner hasn't a clue, isn't listening to my two-suit hand. What shall I bid now – 4♢, 4♡, 3NT?' (They all go down.)

Positive deduction: 'My partner obviously has a string of spades, and a trick outside, perhaps the *club* ace. We should have a good play for 4♠.'

This chapter is a foretaste of things to come. It is designed to make you think. We acknowledge that many players will not make the effort (and good luck to them, too, for essentially bridge is meant to be fun), but we would like you to know where the fascination of bridge lies for the good player.

Jeremy Flint writes, 'I have lost count of the times that I have heard the hoary old fallacy that the expert knows where all the cards are at trick 1. If the opponents haven't bid he knows nothing of the sort. But after a couple of tricks it can be a different story; it may be possible to know the full distribution of the two unseen hands.

'Deduction requires no more than focusing the mind on the problem. It is a lucky photographer who gets the shots he wants without pointing his camera in the right direction.'

To go further would carry us into even deeper waters. The point is this. To begin bridge you require simple arithmetic. To improve you must become aware of the bids and cardplays going on around you. To reach a high level you need to assimilate the evidence, make deductions from it, and come to the most probable assumptions.

None of us can foretell the future, not even what the following day will bring. But if today is scattered with clues we may infer from them that tomorrow is likely to be sunny and bright. Or stormy.

The clues may be difficult to unearth or may be right in front of your eyes. For centuries shepherds have believed, 'Red sky at night, shepherds' delight; red sky in the morning, shepherds' warning.' For all we know they still do. The clue is blazoned across the sky; the deduction (possibly as accurate as that made by the man with the computer and the satellite) that it will be wet or dry the next day; and the conclusion that it would be as well to carry a raincoat—or not.

A tricky job, being a shepherd. Bridge can be tricky too, and beset with problems. It is when you tackle the problems in the right way that it becomes easier. And more fun.

# Glossary

*balanced hand:* a hand in which the suits are evenly distributed. The most balanced hand contains three cards in three suits and four in the other.

*business double:* the same as a penalty double.

*cashing:* cashing tricks means taking them, but with the meaning that a player simply takes the rest of the obvious tricks without searching for extra ones.

*contract:* the final bid, the one which is followed by three passes, is the contract. Making the contract is making the number of tricks promised.

*conventional bid:* an artificial bid with a special meaning, e.g. Blackwood.

*cue bid:* an artificial bid of a suit in search of a slam.

*declarer:* the player who first bids the suit which gains the contract.

*discarding:* when unable to follow suit, throwing a card from another suit.

*distribution* (or shape): how the cards are distributed in a hand according to lengths and shortages.

*double:* a bid which says to opponents that they cannot make their contract. If it succeeds, the penalties are higher; if it fails, the declarer scores higher. A double, in some circumstances, is also a conventional bid.

*doubleton:* two cards only in a suit.

*down:* one down, two down, etc.: one or two tricks short of your contract, incurring a penalty.

*drawing trumps:* taking out opponents' trumps.

*ducking:* deliberately playing a low card when a higher one is available, so giving away a trick in order to gain a later benefit.

*dummy:* partner of the declarer, who takes no part in the play of the hand.

*duplicate:* bridge as played in competitions.

*entries:* high cards which enable a player to get into partner's, or dummy's, hand in order to finesse, play out an established suit, etc.

*establishing:* making a suit good by first, or at some stage, losing a trick or tricks in it.

*finessing:* playing towards split honours, such as A Q, K J; but a finesse can be taken at any level, e.g. through 10 8 in search of the 9.

*forcing bid* (or force): any bid that compels partner to bid again.

*game:* 100 points or more below the line.

*holding up:* purposely not playing a high card when one is available.

*jump bid:* a bid that jumps a level in a new suit, e.g. 1♠–3◇.

*lead:* the first card laid down by a player; the other three play or follow suit to the lead.

*major suits:* spades and hearts.

*minor suits:* diamonds and clubs.

*opener:* the first player to bid.

*overbidding:* bidding too high.

*overcalling:* bidding over an opponent's bid.

*overtricks:* tricks made over and above the number called, and scored above the line.

*part-score:* a score below game-level.

*pass:* the same as no bid; no bid is preferable.

*penalty:* score given away above the line as a result of going down.

*petering:* playing the cards out of order, a higher card to the first trick and a lower one to the second or a later one. A peter is a signal to partner, and is also known as 'playing high–low'.

*playing tricks:* the number of tricks in a hand which can be taken for certain.

*pre-emptive bid:* a high bid on a weak hand, made with the object of interfering with the opponents' bidding.

*quick tricks:* high cards which take tricks quickly. There are only five: an ace is one quick trick, an A K two, a K Q one, A Q one and a half and K x a half.

*raising:* supporting partner's suit at a higher level.

*rebid:* a second or later bid by any player who has already bid once.

*redouble:* a double of a double; it doubles the penalties and the score again. It also has a conventional meaning.

*responder:* partner of the opening bidder.

*reversing:* bidding a higher suit on the second round than the one opened.

*revoking:* failing to follow suit when able to. A revoke carries a penalty.

*rubber:* the best of three games.

*ruffing:* trumping, when having none of the suit led.

*ruff and discard:* the result of a (bad) lead by a defender of a suit of which neither declarer nor dummy has any left; it enables declarer to ruff in one hand and discard a losing card from the other.

*sacrifice bid:* a bid made in the knowledge that the contract will go down, with the object of saving a game for a small penalty.

*safety plays:* plays which limit the number of tricks to be lost, whatever the distribution.

*sequence:* a run of three cards or more, e.g. Q J 10.

*singleton:* one card only in a suit.

*slams:* a small slam is 6 of a suit or 6NTs bid and made; a grand slam 7 of a suit or 7NTs bid and made. Slams carry bonuses.

*table:* playing from the table is synonymous with playing from dummy.

*tenace:* a word describing any split honours, e.g. A Q, K J or any two cards with a middle one missing, such as 10 8.

*void:* none of a suit in a hand.

*vulnerable:* when one partnership has scored a game it becomes vulnerable, and the penalties for going down are higher. At the start of a rubber both sides are non-vulnerable.

*Yarborough:* a hand with no card higher than a 9 in it.